THE
LAW OF
CRIMINAL
INVESTIGATION

THE
LAW OF
CRIMINAL
INVESTIGATION

A Book for
Law Enforcement Personnel

LLOYD L. WEINREB

BALLINGER PUBLISHING COMPANY
Cambridge, Massachusetts
A Subsidiary of Harper and Row, Inc.

PHOTO CREDITS

The Picture Cube, Boston
The photographs on page 2 by Frank Siteman, on page 5 by Peter Baylies, and on page 29 by Eugene Richards.

E.P. Jones Co., Boston
The photographs on pages 47, 73, 135, and 137 by H. Armstrong Roberts.

Stock, Boston, Inc.
The photographs on page 63 by George Malave, on page 70 by Christopher W. Morrow, and on page 133 by Cary Walinsky.

Criminal Justice Publications
The photographs on pp. 86, 136, and 151 by Bernard Edelman, and on page 138 by Bill Powers.

International Standard Book Number: 0–88410–838–4

Library of Congress Catalog Number: 81–7927

Printed in the United States of America

Designed by Virginia J. Mason

Library of Congress Cataloging in Publication Data

Weinreb, Lloyd L., 1936–
    The law of criminal investigation.

    Bibliography: p.
    Includes index.
    1. Criminal investigation—United States. I. Title.
KF9619.W35   345.73'052   81–7927
ISBN 0–88410–838–4   347.30552   AACR2

PREFACE

This book is intended to fill the need of police officers and law enforcement personnel for a clear, accurate guide to the law of criminal investigation. It presents the principles of constitutional law in the context of actual, day-to-day police work, from the point of view of the officer who must decide what to do. Throughout, the emphasis is on the situations confronting the officer rather than technicalities interesting primarily to lawyers who become involved later on.

The constant stream of decisions affecting criminal investigation from the Supreme Court and other federal and state courts has convinced many people that it is impossible to keep abreast of and understand the law. Police officers in particular, whose professional conduct is most directly affected, conclude that the rules are more relevant to legal battles in the courtroom than to the practical realities of law enforcement. The result is that there may seem to be two bodies of law, one for the courts and one for the police, in uneasy coexistence.

There is some justification for this attitude of the police. Many of the Supreme Court's decisions seem to rest on fine distinctions that are hard to discern under the pressure of police duties. Rules defining the authority of the police often are embedded among rules having to do with judicial proceedings, which are of secondary importance to the police but make the answers to the questions that concern them obscure and uncertain. The process of formulating rules in the course of deciding concrete cases makes it inevitable that the hard cases will be more prominent than the much larger number of those falling easily under an established rule.

Nevertheless, there are general principles of constitutional law that apply to crime prevention and criminal investigation. The principles and the reasoning behind them can be stated clearly and simply. They command the assent of a large majority of people in this country. They furnish adequate guidance for the police. And they are adequate to explain the result in most cases. If the facts of a case are too close to the line for a clear decision either way, resort to agreed principles will ordinarily provide a basis for understanding how fair-minded, responsible persons may disagree.

The law of criminal investigation is presented here as much as possible as a set of reasonable, agreed principles, compliance with which police officers should regard as a standard of professional competence. Without disregarding detail when it is important, the book provides a general approach to criminal investigation that will help an officer to act correctly if he is faced with unusual and uncertain circumstances. Every effort is made to show that conscientious adherence to legal principles is not an impediment to effective law enforcement but a part of it.

Topics are arranged according to their place in police work rather than legal rubrics. They include the authority to arrest, stop, or detain a person; the use of force; interference with the movement of a motor vehicle; all aspects of search and seizure; electronic or surreptitious surveillance; booking and investigation at the police station; lineups; and questioning of suspects. A separate chapter discusses the exclusionary rule. Excerpts from or summaries of the facts in leading cases are used to illustrate the impact of a rule in a concrete situation. Aspects of a case that do not affect the choice confronting a police officer are largely left aside. At the end of each chapter, questions and problem cases provide an opportunity for review and further discussion.

I am grateful to the Boston Police Department for permission to include the forms on pp. 24, 50, 134, 138, and 139.

March 1982   L.L.W.

CONTENTS

TABLE OF FORMS

TABLE OF CASES

THE
LAW OF
CRIMINAL
INVESTIGATION

CHAPTER 1

INTRODUCTION

The Police Profession

There are more than 438,000 full-time law enforcement officers in the United States. Together with an additional 121,000 civilian employees, they work in almost 12,000 different agencies of the federal, state, and local governments, which range from a one-officer village police force to the vast, complex bureaucracy of a large city.[1] Some of the details of their work and the manner of its performance vary as much as the setting; an effective officer assigned to a downtown beat relies on skills and experience that would be of little use to an officer responsible for a sparsely populated rural area. For all that diversity, police are united by a common sense of professional identity and purpose.

Like other professional persons, police define their work by the functions they perform. They are responsible for a wide and unpredictable variety of public tasks, loosely held together by a general connection with the peace and order of the community. Much of the work consists of routine operations, like traffic control, on which public safety and well-being depend. Another large aspect of the work is not routine, except insofar as it is always the police who perform it. The police are our public agency of last resort, and often of first resort, for an emergency that calls for swift, forceful, and decisive action.

Most of the situations in which the police are summoned to help do not involve a crime. When a person is injured and regular medical assistance is unavailable, or a child is lost, or a water main bursts, and in countless other circumstances, we turn to the police simply because there is no place else to turn. Such emergencies as well as their routine duties bring the police into constant contact with the public in noncriminal settings.

The most sensational and visible emergency situations are ones involving criminal activity. Not only has someone usually been harmed or endangered. A crime is a direct challenge to public order. It fits well within the general context of their work, therefore, that the police have primary responsibility for the prevention of crime, by intervening to frustrate its success and minimize the harm if they can or by investigating and apprehending the criminal, so that the criminal law can be applied. No other task is so readily associated with them. The police encourage this image of themselves as crimefighters, public officials who wage the community's battles against crime.

Crime control differs significantly from other kinds of police work. In noncriminal emergencies and on routine patrol, the police are present mainly to give assistance. When they respond to the scene of an accident, for example, the persons there are glad to see them and willingly cooperate. That is true also, of course, of one aspect of the response to a crime. The victim of a mugging who lies injured on the street or the householder who has returned to a burgled home measures police effectiveness by the speed with which they appear and is eager for them to take charge.

The criminal, however, is anything but glad to see the police. Far from encouraging their work, his objective is precisely opposed to theirs; the more obstacles in their way, to make their work more difficult and prevent its success, the better. The criminal is sometimes described as the "client" of the police. If so, no one should be misled into believing that he is a client who seeks their services.

Criminal Investigation

This book is about the law of criminal investigation. We shall study the rules that give the police authority to investigate crime and apprehend criminals and, at the same time, set the limits of that authority. As every officer knows, investigative tasks cannot be neatly separated from direct crime prevention or ordinary peace-keeping. Often, therefore, we shall touch also on aspects of police work that are not strictly investigative. Among the topics that we shall consider are when an officer can stop a person whose behavior is suspicious and ask for an account of his actions; when it is lawful to make an arrest; when it is lawful to search a person, or his suitcase, or car, or house; how to conduct a lineup; and when and how a criminal suspect can be questioned about a crime.

We shall not be much concerned, except incidentally, with investigative technique as it is discussed in some training manuals: methods of identification or interrogation and the like that have proven to be successful. We shall be discussing technique in another, more important sense. For unless rules of law are observed, the most "successful" investigative methods may fail because their results are not admissible in evidence. Even if the admission of evidence is not a primary concern, a responsible investigator carries out his work as authorized by law—just as a good businessman is one who earns high profits within the law and not in violation of it. It is not good police work to apprehend a suspect, even if he is guilty, or to obtain evidence, even if it is highly material, by unlawful means.

Police Authority

The law of criminal investigation reflects the peculiar antagonistic relationship between police and the criminal. While officers ordinarily rely on the willing cooperation of others, when they encounter someone who is or may be a criminal they rely on their *authority* to *require* his cooperation, whether he is willing or not. Sometimes a suspect does cooperate with an appearance of willingness, hoping not to be incriminated; if it turns out otherwise, he is likely to claim (and in retrospect, to believe) that he cooperated against his will. Whatever the appearance at the time, when the investigation of a crime involves a person who may be the criminal, it usually rests on an officer's authority to take certain actions without regard to the person's own wishes. This antagonism is the more difficult because the officer often has to assert his authority swiftly and suddenly, with enough force to make it effective, before there is time to study the situation carefully. Even if he is sensitive to the limitations on his authority, in a true emergency when innocent persons may be hurt, he cannot wait to be certain. Good police work may require him to act first and ask questions later.

It would, perhaps, be a simple solution to give officers unlimited authority and instruct them to rely on cooperation if possible but to act without it if necessary. A society in which *government under law* is a first, basic principle cannot allow public officials to act in that way. Even a social objective as important as controlling crime cannot be pursued without restraint. Each of us has liberties that the government protects from interference by its own officials.

When one hears of a case in which a criminal "got away" because the court concluded that an officer exceeded his authority, it is easy to think that the rules of law interfere with the functions officers are expected to perform: "On the one hand, you tell us to catch criminals. On the other hand, you won't let us do what we need to do to catch them." The rules that we shall examine are the source of an officer's authority as well as the limits on it. The limits are only the boundaries of the authority that the law itself confers. The authority of the police is not limited for the purpose of giving the criminal a break. Rather, it is limited because, along with law and order, we value other features of our community life as well. In the troubling circumstances of a crime, we may not be able to satisfy them all fully.

In most circumstances, the authority of the police is well suited to the performance of their duties. Sometimes it is reasonable to argue that the law is too restrictive or that, even if the law is sound in principle, its application in a particular case was unsound and that somewhat greater authority should have been allowed. So long as one recalls that there may be an opposing view, which is

5

also reasonably held, it is entirely proper to discuss critically rules of law and their application. Police officers, like other public officials, have the right and the responsibility to discuss the rules of law that affect their work and to criticize rules that seem impractical or unwise. The community has need of the knowledge and experience of the experts on whom it relies for law enforcement and will listen to their views.

Uniform Law

Unlike most countries, the United States does not have a national police force directed and supervised from one central office. Police departments are agencies of local government, and their loyalties and responsibilities are local. There are a few national and state police agencies, like the FBI and state highway patrols, but they are exceptions and typically have a special, limited jurisdiction. Criminal investigation is mostly the work of the local departments, which have working arrangements with one another but are administered independently.

Even so, it is not inaccurate to refer to a uniform national law that applies to all police agencies and establishes the main principles of criminal investigation. As one people, we are committed to a common understanding of the fundamental relationship between the government and individuals. We agree about the liberties and freedom from unnecessary official intrusions that individuals ordinarily expect and to which they are entitled, as we agree about the importance of law and order. These shared values are general enough to permit marked local variations. They have their own significance, nonetheless.

There is a still stronger source of uniformity. Starting around 1960, provisions of the Constitution affecting criminal investigation have been applied to state and federal police work, in enough detail to provide a set of rules common to both. Most of the rules have been derived from a small number of provisions contained in the Fourth, Fifth, and Sixth Amendments of the Bill of Rights, which the courts interpret and apply in criminal cases. Those rules and their constitutional basis are the main subject of this book.

Courts do not have general authority to enact laws or make rules. For that, we rely on legislatures and administrative agencies of government. Courts do, however, apply the law when they try cases of persons accused of crime. It is a long-settled doctrine of our law that if there is a conflict between a provision of the Constitution, as the highest law in the land, and any other law, the Constitution prevails. Because the Constitution is superior to any other authority of the police or prosecutor, when a person is prosecuted in a state or federal court, any evidence against him that was obtained in violation of his constitutional rights cannot be used and is excluded from the trial.

We shall examine this "exclusionary rule" closely in the next chapter. Its effect is that whenever a criminal defendant objects to the prosecutor's use of evidence and claims that it was obtained in violation of his constitutional rights, the court conducting the trial has to decide whether the Constitution allows officers to behave as they did in that instance. If the defendant's claim is rejected, and he is convicted and appeals from the conviction, the reviewing court also has to consider his constitutional claim. So, if police search and find stolen goods, or question a suspect and he makes an incriminating admission, or in any of the other situations in which evidence is obtained, the method of investigation has to meet the constitutional standard. By ruling in thousands of cases whether a particular piece of evidence is admissible, the Supreme Court and lower courts have declared how criminal investigation is to be conducted.

There is nothing to prevent a state or city or an individual police department from giving officers *less* authority than the Constitution allows. Courts have no occasion to interfere if a proper governmental body concludes that the authority of police should be limited even further, since there is no violation of constitutional rights. In theory, therefore, even though the Constitution applies uniformly, we might have many different bodies of state law. In practice, the states and local governments have generally allowed the police the full extent of their constitutional authority. Local variations mostly concern less important matters of procedure and technical detail.

While a police officer has to know and abide by local rules, an error in this respect seldom is as serious or has as serious consequences as a violation of the Constitution.

Our reliance on case-by-case, judicial decisions for the most important rules defining police investigative authority may sometimes make it difficult to perceive general legal principles. Officers may struggle with opinions of the Supreme Court and other courts and conclude that the results depend on hair-splitting distinctions that they cannot apply meaningfully to their own work. They may wonder how they can be expected to understand and follow rules about which judges themselves often disagree.

Although it is true that some of the cases discussed in judicial opinions turn on refined analysis of small factual distinctions, these are a small fraction of the criminal cases that courts hear and adjudicate easily by straightforward application of well-known and easily understood rules. In the myriad circumstances of police work, difficult cases presenting facts close to the constitutional line cannot be avoided. Officers will find it helpful to study such a case as an application of and an aid to understanding a general rule rather than merely as the pronouncement of a narrow rule applicable only to the precise facts at issue. So, for example, if a court announces that an officer making an arrest lawfully searched a paper bag in the possession of the arrested person but that his search of a small suitcase was unlawful (see pp. 73-76 below), officers should consider that not simply as a rule about paper bags and small suitcases but as an explanation of the large general principles protective of individual privacy that are embodied in the Fourth Amendment. The many discussions of particular cases in this book will help officers to take that approach to legal material.

The case-by-case development of the law should have special attraction to police officers engaged in daily operations of great and unpredictable variety. Rules are fashioned in the context of actual, concrete circumstances, in which the needs of law enforcement and criminal investigation are vividly presented. Whether or not they approve of the result in a particular case, officers can be certain that the demands of professional police work are reflected in the law.

Questions for Discussion

1. **The police profession.**   It is not unusual for members of a profession to see their role differently from the way that others see it. Because police officers come into contact with so many different people in such diverse and often tense and uncomfortable circumstances, it is especially important that they be able to see themselves as others see them. For a start, describe the police profession precisely and fully, from your own point of view. Then describe the profession from the point of view of others, including the following (and any others whose points of view you think would be significantly different):

    i.   *The victim of a housebreaking.*   Items of considerable value have been taken. He has called the police and is waiting anxiously when they arrive.

    ii. *The victim of a mugging on the street.*   Her purse has been taken. She is lying on the ground and is nearly hysterical when an officer on patrol duty arrives at the scene.

    iii. *A witness to the mugging described above.* He saw a man grab the woman's purse and run off. When the officer arrives, the witness is talking to the woman and trying to calm her.

    iv. *A man who is stopped near the scene of the mugging.*   The officer who stops him suspects that he may have committed the mugging. Consider two cases: (a) the officer's suspicion is in fact correct; (b) the officer's suspicion is not correct.

    v.   *A person who is arrested for murder.*   He claims that he shot the victim in self-defense, after the victim had attacked him with a knife.

    In each of the cases, what functions is an officer on the scene expected to perform?
    In performing those functions, to what extent can the officer rely on willing cooperation and to what extent must he rely on his authority?

2. **Rules and regulations.**   Give examples of different kinds of rules and regulations that apply to you in the conduct of your assignments.
    What is their source?
    Which ones do you take most seriously? Somewhat seriously? Not so seriously?

How do you account for the difference?
What is the consequence of a failure to comply with
each of them?

Notes

1. The exact figures as of October 31, 1980, were 438,442 full-time law-enforcement officers and 121,474 full-time civilian employees, reported by 11,719 agencies. The national rate was 2.1 officers and 2.7 total law-enforcement employees per 1,000 inhabitants. U.S. Department of Justice, FBI Uniform Crime Reports, Crime in the United States 1980 (1981), p. 260.

CHAPTER 2

THE EXCLUSIONARY RULE

Most of the rules of law affecting the conduct of criminal investigation and the apprehension of a criminal were fashioned by the courts. We noted in the last chapter how that occurs: in countless criminal cases, courts apply the rule that evidence obtained in violation of the defendant's constitutional rights cannot be used against him. In this chapter we shall examine this "exclusionary rule" and consider the arguments for and against it.

Mapp v. Ohio

Three police officers went to the home of a woman named Dollree Mapp. They had information that a person who was involved in a recent bombing was hiding there and that policy paraphernalia was also hidden. Mapp and her daughter lived on the upper floor of a two-family house. The officers demanded to be admitted. Mapp, having talked to her lawyer on the telephone, refused to admit them without a search warrant. The officers maintained surveillance of the house for about three hours. Then, with four or more additional officers on the scene, they again sought entrance. Mapp did not admit them, and they broke in. Her lawyer arrived; the officers did not allow him to enter the house. Mapp appeared on the stairs to the upper floor and asked to see a search warrant. An officer held up a piece of paper, which she grabbed. The officers struggled with her and retrieved the paper. They

put handcuffs on her and forcibly brought her back to her
apartment. The apartment and the basement of the house
were searched thoroughly. In a trunk in the basement,
police found some obscene materials. She was prosecuted
for their possession.[1]

The officers who broke into Mapp's home had no
search warrant. (Whatever paper they had shown her
later disappeared; it was not a warrant.) The forcible
entry and search were plainly unlawful; they violated
Mapp's rights under the Fourth Amendment (see Chapter
8). At her trial, the prosecutor offered in evidence the
materials found in the basement during the search. Mapp
objected.

Should the evidence that the police obtained unlawfully be used against Mapp?
How do you explain your answer?

The Supreme Court's answer was that the evidence
should not be used. The prosecutor could not rely on
evidence to convict Mapp if the police violated her
constitutional rights when they obtained it. The crime
that was charged against Mapp does not seem very
serious; it was only that she had possession of a small
amount of pornographic material: as one of the Justices
said, "four little pamphlets, a couple of photographs and
a little pencil doodle."[2] The rule applies, however, no
matter how serious the crime and no matter how crucial
to a conviction the evidence may be.

Several defenses of the rule have been given. To the
extent that officers might otherwise deliberately or carelessly violate a person's rights in order to obtain evidence
of guilt, exclusion may act as a deterrent to such lawless-
ness by removing the motive for it. Second, even if a
violation was not deliberate or careless, exclusion does
no more than treat the situation as if no violation had
occurred. The rule does not mean that the person whose
rights were violated cannot be prosecuted and convicted.
Only evidence that the government would not have had
except for the violation is excluded. All evidence that is
lawfully obtained can be used. Third, if a court were to
receive evidence obtained unlawfully, it would appear to

condone lawless police conduct. Whether one looks at the rule prospectively, as a deterrent to future violations, or retrospectively, as a correction of violations that have occurred, the core of its justification is the respect that public officials must have for constitutional rights.

Arguments against the exclusionary rule begin with the observation that it impedes the effort to discover the facts at trial, because reliable evidence of guilt cannot be used. It is not an effective deterrent to unlawful police conduct, critics say, either because such conduct usually is not deliberate or, if it is deliberate, has objectives other than obtaining evidence for use at trial, such as clearing the case. If officers are unaware that their conduct is unlawful or do not care whether evidence is admitted or not, the threat of exclusion will not deter them. Noting the difficulties that the courts themselves have in deciding many close cases, the critics ask how officers can be expected not to make mistakes.

Criticism of the retrospective ground for exclusion is summed up in a well-known phrase: Why should "the criminal...go free because the constable has blundered"?[3] If an officer violates the law, it is argued, we should deal directly with that violation rather than give the criminal a lucky break. To this argument one might reply that the criminal does not go free *because* the officer violated the law. He may still be prosecuted and convicted if there is enough lawfully obtained evidence; at Mapp's trial, for example, the prosecutor was prevented only from using the evidence that the officers had found in the trunk and seized unlawfully. It has also been observed that, whether or not the exclusionary rule is a very effective response to a violation of constitutional law, there is no other response that is likely to be more effective.

Other countries do not apply a general rule of exclusion as we do. Their courts ordinarily receive any evidence that is relevant and reliable, without regard to the manner in which it was obtained. However, the tradition of personal, specific, and enforceable constitutional rights, out of which the exclusionary rule grows, is especially strong in this country. Also, other countries commonly have stronger central administrative direction of the police, which may make alternative responses more effective.

Criticism of the exclusionary rule has been strong,

including even some criticism by Justices of the Supreme Court. Its defense has also been strong. Whatever one's own conclusions, the rule is an established part of American constitutional law. It is the principal means by which constitutional rights in the law of criminal investigation have been developed.

Scope of the Exclusionary Rule

In the *Mapp* case, the excluded evidence was a direct product of the search that violated Mapp's rights. Often, the connection between the evidence and the allegedly illegal action of the police is not so close. For example, suppose that instead of finding obscene materials on the premises the officers had found a notebook containing an address where obscene materials belonging to Mapp were found in a subsequent search, which did not itself violate her rights. Or suppose that Mapp had been arrested unlawfully and had made remarks to the arresting officer that incriminated her in an unrelated crime. Should her remarks be excluded as the product of the illegal arrest? Or should the arrest and the remarks be treated as separate?

A partial answer to the problem of applying the exclusionary rule in such situations was provided by *Wong Sun v. United States*,[4] a case decided two years after *Mapp*. The test, the court said, was not simply whether the police would not have obtained the evidence "but for" their illegal act. Were that the test, evidence would be excluded too often, even when there was only a remote connection between the illegal act and the evidence. Instead, one has to ask also whether events intervening between the illegal act and the obtaining of evidence had so weakened the connection between them that the "taint" of the illegality was dissipated before the evidence was obtained.

Such a test is not one that can be applied with precision. On the one hand, the purposes of the exclusionary rule do not require that all evidence connected in any way, however insignificant, with prior illegal police behavior be excluded. On the other hand, officers should not be able to evade the rule by using the product of an illegal act to obtain other evidence safeguarded from exclusion. From the large number of such cases that have been decided, some general propositions emerge:

1. *If officers obtain evidence of certain facts by conduct that violated the defendant's constitutional rights, the same facts can be proved by other evidence lawfully obtained from an independent source.* For example, officers search the defendant's house unlawfully and seize articles of clothing that help to identify him as the criminal. Without knowing about the unlawful search, a member of the defendant's household voluntarily delivers to the police other articles of clothing that also help the witness to identify him. The unlawfully seized clothing cannot be used in evidence against the defendant. The other articles can be used, even though they are used to prove the same facts that would have been proved by the unlawfully seized clothing. Or, officers arrest the defendant unlawfully and obtain his fingerprints. At his trial, fingerprints found at the scene of the crime are matched against another set of his prints already lawfully on record. The unlawful arrest does not prevent identification of the defendant by the latter source.[5]

2. *If officers learn the name of a witness by an illegal act, the witness will be allowed to testify against the defendant if the testimony is a product of the witness's own decision and not a direct result of the illegality.* In one case, an officer illegally looked inside an envelope in the defendant's shop; the contents of the envelope incriminated the defendant. Months later, an employee in the shop was interviewed and agreed to testify against the defendant. The subject of the interview and her testimony at trial were related to the contents of the envelope. The testimony was held to be admissible, because the purpose of the illegal search was not to find a witness, a substantial time passed after the search before the witness was interviewed, the identity of the witness and her connection with the defendant were known independently of the search, and she testified freely and voluntarily. The Supreme Court concluded that in those circumstances, the taint of the illegal search was dissipated and the witness's testimony was not a product of the illegality.[6] But in another case, where officers conducted an illegal search to obtain evidence against the defendant and discovered the name of a previously unknown witness who testified unwillingly, it was held that the testimony was a direct product of the search and not admissible.[7]

3. *If a person is arrested unlawfully, then is released and consults with his lawyer, and later makes incriminating statements to the police, the statements are admissible, even though he would not have made them but for the illegal arrest.* His release after the arrest and the time for reflection and consultation with a lawyer break the connection between the unlawful arrest and the statements.

4.   *If officers purposely commit an illegal act in order to obtain evidence, the evidence is not admissible.*   For example, knowing that it is unlawful, officers arrest a person in the hope that he will make an incriminating statement. Any statement that he makes is not admissible against him.

5.   *If the police exploit an illegal act in order to gain evidence, even if that was not their original purpose the evidence is not admissible.*   For example, having made an arrest that they believe is lawful, officers question the person closely during the period of detention. The arrest turns out to have been unlawful. Any statement that he makes is not admissible against him.

6.   *In general, the longer and more complicated the chain of events between an illegal act of the police and the discovery of evidence, the more likely it is that the evidence is admissible; the simpler and more direct the connection between the illegal act and the evidence, the more likely it is that the evidence will be excluded.*   For example, if a person who has been unlawfully arrested makes statements that furnish the basis for an otherwise lawful search and that search in turn produces evidence that furnishes a basis for a subsequent lawful search, the evidence obtained by each succeeding action is less closely connected with the original illegality and is more likely to be admitted.

As the above propositions and examples indicate, an officer who becomes aware that a suspect's constitutional rights may have been violated does not need to fear that prosecution will be frustrated altogether. He should carefully consider the extent of the illegality and take appropriate measures to insulate it from further investigative steps still to be taken. So far as practicable, he should avoid using it as a lead to further evidence. When a mistake is discovered, the professional response is to correct it. An officer who acts promptly to remedy even a possible constitutional violation will assist a subsequent prosecution far more than one who disregards it and hopes that it will turn out to be alright.

Standing

The exclusion of evidence obtained in violation of a person's constitutional rights is a remedy for the wrong done to that person. While one of the purposes of the rule is to deter such violations in the future, that deterrent effect is to be achieved only as part of the remedy for the individual wrong. Only a person whose own rights have been violated has "standing" to suppress evidence obtained by the violation. If the defendant is someone else—a "third person"—the evidence is admissible.

In one case, officers investigating drug offenses searched the purse of a woman named Cox. A friend of hers, Rawlings, had asked her to keep some drugs in the purse for him. Rawlings was prosecuted for possession of the drugs. At his trial, he sought to exclude from evidence the drugs found in Cox's purse, on the ground that the search was unlawful. The Supreme Court concluded that whether the search was lawful or not, it invaded no rights of Rawlings; only Cox herself had standing to challenge the lawfulness of the search, and she was not the defendant. Accordingly, the drugs were admissible at Rawling's trial.[8]

Supporters of the exclusionary rule sometimes oppose this limitation on it. They argue that a defendant should be able to object to the use of any evidence that was obtained in violation of the Constitution, even if his own rights were not violated. The deterrent effect of the exclusionary rule is the same in both cases, and, it is urged, the courts should not appear to condone illegal police conduct, no matter whose rights were violated. These arguments have not prevailed. There would probably be little extra deterrence if the requirement of standing were eliminated. More generally, the exclusionary rule was developed as, and is still perceived as, a means of redress for a person whose rights have been violated. From that point of view, the requirement makes sense.

It has sometimes been suggested that officers might exploit the requirement of standing by violating A's rights in order to uncover evidence against B and violating B's rights in order to uncover evidence against A. A deliberate scheme of that sort would not go unchecked by the courts. More to the point, it is the responsibility of police conscientiously to honor constitutional rights as part of the law that they uphold and enforce. Even if it were possible to avoid the exclusion of evidence, it is unprofessional and improper for an officer knowingly or carelessly to violate the Constitution. While he ought to understand the operation of the exclusionary rule and the reasons for it, his principle concern is to act according to the law. If an officer does that to the best of his ability, he need have no fear that evidence produced by his labors will be lost in court.

Questions for Discussion

1. What is the "exclusionary rule"?
    To which crimes does it apply?

2. What arguments support the exclusionary rule?
    What responses are there?

3. What are the arguments against the exclusionary rule?
    What responses are there?

4. Is all evidence that would not have been found but for an illegal official act excluded from evidence?
    What general principle applies?
    What rules have been developed for application of the principle?

5. Why is evidence obtained illegally excluded only at the trial of a person whose own constitutional rights were violated?

Problem Cases

The following cases provide an opportunity to study the application of the exclusionary rule. Study the facts of each case and consider what arguments you might make in favor of or against the exclusion of evidence. Remember that these are not questions for which there is necessarily one right answer. It is as important to be able to explain your answer and to understand arguments on the other side as it is to come up with the answer itself.

After you have decided whether the evidence should be excluded in the actual case, consider what the police officer(s) should have done to make certain that valuable evidence would not be lost.

1. Acting on a tip from another narcotics user, federal narcotics agents went to James Toy's shop to arrest him for possession of narcotics. When he learned who the agents were, Toy ran to his living quarters in the rear. The agents chased him and arrested him in the bedroom. The arrest was unlawful because there was not probable cause for Toy's arrest (see Chapter 3). In response to the agents' questions in the bedroom, Toy named John Yee as a user of narcotics. The agents went to Yee's house and arrested him. He surrendered a quantity of narcotics. Toy and Yee were taken to the office of the Bureau of Narcotics. There Yee said that he had been given the narcotics a few days earlier by Toy and another man. Toy identified the other man as Wong Sun and told the agents where Wong Sun lived. The agents went to the house and arrested him. All three were taken before a magistrate, charged with narcotics violations, and subsequently released. Within the next few days all three were interrogated at the Bureau office after having been advised of their rights.[9]

At the trials of Toy, Yee, and Wong Sun, should any of the following evidence be excluded: (1) Toy's statement to the agents in his bedroom; (2) the narcotics taken from Yee at his house; (3) Toy's statements during the interrogation at the Bureau office; (4) Wong Sun's statements during the interrogation at the Bureau office?

2. An agent of the Immigration and Naturalization Service obtained a warrant to search the Steve's Pier One Restaurant for aliens illegally in this country. INS agents made the search and found seven illegal aliens, who were arrested. The owner of the restaurant and his brother, who was a chef, were prosecuted for harboring and concealing the aliens. The search of the restaurant was unlawful because the warrant was issued without probable cause (see Chapter 8). The defendants made a motion to exclude from their trial any evidence of the presence of the aliens at the restaurant that was obtained during the illegal search and also any testimony of the aliens who were found during the search.[10]

How should the trial judge rule on the motion?

Notes

1. Mapp v. Ohio, 367 U.S. 643 (1961).

2. Id. at 666, 668 (concurring opinion of Justice Douglas).

3. The phrase, which is often quoted, is in an opinion of Justice (then Judge) Cardozo in People v. Defore, 242 N.Y. 13, 21, 150 N.E. 585, 587 (1926).

4. 371 U.S. 471 (1963). Many of the facts of the case are set forth in problem (1), at the end of the chapter, p. 19.

5. The facts described are those of Bynum v. United States, 274 F.2d 767 (D.C. Cir. 1960).

6. United States v. Ceccolini, 435 U.S. 268 (1978).

7. United States v. Scios, 590 F.2d 956 (D.C. Cir. 1978).

8. Rawlings v. Kentucky, 448 U.S. 98 (1980).

9. Wong Sun v. United States, 371 U.S. 471 (1963).

10. See United States v. Karathanos, 531 F.2d 26 (2d Cir. 1976).

CHAPTER 3

ARREST

This chapter discusses the authority of police officers to make an arrest. No aspect of their work is so readily associated with them in the public mind. To the extent that we think of police as crimefighters, that association is correct. Not only does the authority to arrest determine

when police can take someone into custody for commission of a crime; often an arrest is also the means by which police carry out an investigation. As we shall see in later chapters, the validity of a search of a person as well as procedures carried out at the police station, like an identification lineup, usually depend on a prior lawful arrest.

There are at least three perspectives from which an arrest can be viewed: that of the police officer, who sees it as the performance of some function; that of the person arrested, who is concerned about the interference with his ordinary liberty; and that of the judge, who has to determine the lawfulness of the arrest by applying general constitutional principles to the particular circumstances. How one describes an arrest often depends a good deal on the perspective from which one is looking.

The Fourth Amendment

Authority to arrest is bounded by the Fourth Amendment to the Constitution:

> *The right of the people to be secure in their persons, houses, papers, and effects, against unreasonable searches and seizures, shall not be violated, and no warrants shall issue, but upon probable cause, supported by oath or affirmation, and particularly describing the place to be searched, and the persons or things to be seized.*

There is not much in those few words to indicate the details of the law affecting an officer's authority to stop or arrest someone. One might think that another provision of the Constitution, the declaration that no person shall be deprived of liberty without due process of law,[1] is more obviously concerned with authority to arrest. It is, however, an accepted part of American constitutional law that the security of the person protected by the Fourth Amendment covers ordinary police actions that interfere with a person's liberty. Accordingly, the law of arrest is based on interpretation of the language of the Amendment.

Arrest

In a wide variety of situations, so common that we scarcely notice them, the police have authority to regulate public behavior as a direct consequence of their responsibility to ensure public safety and order. No one questions an officer's authority to keep people back from the scene of an accident or to divert them away from a broken water main. An officer directing traffic at an intersection stops cars going one way while the cross traffic proceeds. Even though the freedom of movement of the drivers in the stopped cars is temporarily impeded, we do not ask whether the officer acts within his authority, because he could not direct traffic otherwise. A failure to respect his authority would itself be a violation of the law.

In such situations, we do not think of the police action as having deprived a person of his liberty. Whatever exercise of authority the occasion may demand, the interference is as small and as brief as the circumstances permit; usually, as long as the person refrains from conduct that would aggravate the emergency, he can do as he likes. Sometimes, however, an officer takes an action directed at a particular person, who is no longer free to go where he chooses; the very purpose of the officer's action is to interrupt that person's freedom of movement. The authority of police to take that kind of action is defined much more carefully than their general role as keepers of the peace. Not limited to the protection of public order and safety and directed at a particular person, such action affects the ordinary right of an individual in our society to be at liberty, to do as he pleases. No more than any other official, can a police officer take such action without restraint.

Often it is difficult to distinguish between the two kinds of action, and it is unnecessary. Arriving at the scene of what looks like a mugging, an officer may have to take swift action on the basis of a moment's observation. If he sees someone rapidly leaving the scene, he may have to stop the person at least until the officer learns what has happened. If it turns out that no crime has been committed or that the person before him is not the criminal, the encounter will end there. Ordinarily, neither the officer nor the person whom he briefly stopped will describe the incident as an arrest. Most of us, police and

Boston Police
INCIDENT REPORT

HANDPRINT

ORIGINAL ☐   SUPPLEMENTARY ☐

01. KEY SITUATIONS	02. COMPLAINT NO.	03. REPORT DIST.	CLEARANCE DIST.	PAGE	OF
☐ DRUGS ☐ LICENSED PREMISES ☐ ELDERLY ☐ JUVENILE ☐ COMMUNITY DISORDERS ☐ OTHER					

04. TYPE OF INCIDENT	05. CRIME CODE	06. STATUS ☐ INACTIVE ☐ UNFOUNDED ☐ ARREST ☐ UNDER 18) ☐ EXCEPT CL ☐ UNDER 18)	07. DATE OF OCCUR. A.	B.

08. LOCATION OF INCIDENT (NO. STREET) (INTERSECTION—ALPHA ORDER)	APT.	09. DISPATCH TIME ☐ A ☐ P	10. TIME OF OCCUR. ☐ A ☐ P A. B.	☐ A ☐ P

11. VICTIM-COMP. (LAST, FIRST, M.I.)	12. PHONE	13. SEX ☐ M ☐ F	14. RACE	15. MARITAL STATUS ☐ MARRIED ☐ UNMARRIED

16. ADDRESS (NO., STREET, CITY AND STATE IF OTHER THAN BOSTON OR MASS.)	APT.	OCCUPATION	17. AGE	18. D.O.B.

19. PERSON REPORTING (IF DIFFERENT THAN ABOVE)	20. ADDRESS	APT.	21. PHONE

22. WAS THERE A WITNESS TO THE CRIME

PERSON INTERVIEWED	AGE	LOCATION OF INTERVIEW	APT. NO.	HOME ADDRESS	APT.	TEL	RES. BUS.

A ☐ ☐ YES NO

23. NUMBER OF PERPETRATORS | CAN SUSPECT BE IDENTIFIED AT THIS TIME

B ☐ ☐ YES NO

PERSONS

24. ☐ ARREST ☐ MISSING ☐ WARRANT ☐ SUSPECT ☐ SUMMONS	25. NAME (LAST, FIRST, M.I.)	26. S.S. NO.	27. BOOKING NO.	28. PHOTO NO.	29. ALIAS
30. WARRANT NO.	31. ADDRESS		32. SEX ☐ M ☐ F	33. RACE	34. AGE	35. HEIGHT	36. D.O.B.
37. SPECIAL CHARACTERISTICS (INCLUDE CLOTHING)			38. WEIGHT	39. BUILD	40. HAIR	41. EYES

42. CAN SUSPECT VEHICLE BE DESCRIBED

C ☐ ☐ YES NO

VEHICLES

43. ☐ STOLEN ☐ RECOV. ☐ LV. SCENE ☐ ABAND. ☐ IN CUST. ☐ TOWED ☐ USED IN CRIME ☐ OTHER	44. REG. STATE NO.	45. PLATE TYPE YEAR (EXP.)	46. MODEL
47. VEHICLE MAKE-YEAR	48. VEHICLE ID NO.	49. STYLE	50. COLOR (TOP-BOTTOM)
51. OPERATOR'S NAME	52. LICENSE NO.	53. OPERATOR'S ADDRESS	
54. OWNER'S NAME	55. OWNER'S ADDRESS		

56. CAN PROPERTY BE IDENTIFIED

D ☐ ☐ YES NO

PROPERTY

57. TYPE OF PROPERTY	58. SERIAL OR I-DENTI-GUARD NO.	59. BRAND NAME-DESCRIPTION	60. MODEL	61. VALUE	62. UCR	63. RECOV

64. IS THERE A SIGNIFICANT M.O.

E ☐ ☐ YES NO

MO

65. TYPE OF WEAPON-TOOL	66. NEIGHBORHOOD	67. TYPE OF BUILDING	68. PLACE OF ENTRY
69. WEATHER	70. LIGHTING	71. TRANSPORTATION OF SUSPECT (CAR, FOOT, MBTA, ETC.)	72. VICTIM'S ACTIVITY
73. UNUSUAL ACTIONS AND STATEMENTS OF PERPETRATOR			RELATIONSHIP TO VICTIM

74. IS THERE ANY PHYSICAL EVIDENCE (DESCRIPTION AND DISPOSITION IN NARRATIVE)

F ☐ ☐

75. IS THERE ANY OTHER REASON FOR FURTHER INVESTIGATION (REASON BELOW)

G ☐ ☐
YES NO

BLOCK NO.	76. NARRATIVE AND ADDITIONAL INFORMATION

SOLVABILITY FACTOR

77. UNIT ASSIGNED	78. TOUR OF DUTY	79. REPORTING OFFICER'S SIGNATURE	80. REPORTING OFFICER'S I.D	81. PARTNER'S I.D.	F.I. ☐ YES ☐ NO
82. DATE OF REPORT	83. SPECIAL UNITS NOTIFIED (REPORTING)				TELETYPE NO.
84. TIME COMPLETED ☐ A ☐ P	85. SIGNATURE OF PATROL SUPERVISOR	86. PAT. SUP. ID.	87. SIGNATURE DUTY SUPERVISOR	88. DUTY SUP. ID.

BPD Form 1.1 Revised 79

HEADQUARTER'S RECORD

public alike, think an arrest includes being taken to the station house and booked before being released. From the constitutional point of view, a seizure of the person has occurred from the moment when an officer takes action so that a person is no longer free to go as he pleases. With few exceptions, such seizures are treated as arrests, which the police are authorized to make only under certain circumstances.

An arrest is lawful only if the arresting officer has probable cause to believe that the person arrested is committing or has committed a crime.

That basic principle of constitutional law is the most important single rule for a police officer to know. It applies to a broad range of police activity. In the rest of this chapter and in succeeding chapters, we shall study the rule and its applications in detail.

Pendergrast v. United States

Shortly after midnight, two men walking along the sidewalk were attacked. A wallet, watch, and money were taken from one of them and a watch and penknife from the other. Police officers arrived at the scene within a few minutes. A small crowd of spectators had gathered. One of the victims pointed to Pendergrast, who was standing among the spectators, and told the police that Pendergrast was one of the men who had attacked him. The other man who had been mugged had left the scene. The victim was bruised and excited and admitted that he had been drinking before the incident; but he insisted that his identification of Pendergrast, who was a stranger to him, was correct. An officer went up to Pendergrast and asked what he was doing in the area. He replied that he had just left a party and was taking a walk to get some air. The officer informed him of the accusation, which he denied.[2]

Figure 3-1.
Incident Report

Ellis v. United States

"...[O]fficers...had been specially assigned to look for the perpetrator of a series of day-time housebreakings that had taken place in a particular area in Northeast Washington. ...[T]he Police Department had broadcast many descriptions of the suspect ('look-outs'), the latest having been issued on the day prior to the arrest. The look-outs—based on information received from complaining witnesses—described the suspect as a 'brown-skinned' colored man about 'five feet seven' or 'five feet eight' in height, about 150 pounds in weight, 'very neatly' dressed, wearing a 'gray topcoat,' sometimes said to have a 'half-belt' in the back, or a 'black topcoat,' and a 'brown' or 'gray' hat. His age was variously described as 'middle teens,' 'late teens,' '19, 21, 22,' or '22–24.' The look-outs, issued from time to time over a period of months, referred to each of a series of crimes of common pattern, all having been committed by someone who forced open the front doors of houses, with some instrument, in the daylight hours.

"On the day in question, shortly before noon, the officers, who were in plain clothes, were driving an unmarked car down one of the streets in the area where the crimes had occurred. They saw Ellis approach on foot from the opposite direction. They testified they were mindful of the descriptions given in the look-outs, and that Ellis appeared to them to be the wanted man: he was 'brown-skinned,' 'around five seven or five eight' in height, from 'a hundred forty-five to a hundred and fifty' pounds in weight, 'very neatly dressed,' wearing a 'gray topcoat with a half-belt in the back,' and 'brown' hat, and was estimated to be 'between twenty-two and twenty-five' years old.

"The officers drove on a short distance, turned their car around, and waited. They saw Ellis go up on the porch of a house, knock on the door, stand there looking 'around the area' for a 'few minutes,' then return to the street and walk back toward the direction from which he had come. As Ellis approached, the officers hailed him and asked him to come to their car, saying that they were police officers. They got out of the car, and asked Ellis his name. He gave it. He was then asked, 'Do you have any identification?' The answer was in the negative. Ellis appeared nervous; he 'dropped his money...chewing gum, cigarettes, and so forth on the ground.' The officers 'asked him twice to take his hand out of his pocket.' However, he 'kept his right hand in his coat pocket and his arm close against his side.' One of the officers 'patted him and found a bulge in his inside pocket on the righthand side.' "[3]

In *Pendergrast*, no one doubts that the officers who came to the scene of the mugging had authority to keep the spectators back from the injured man on the ground. If someone had been foolish enough to insist on approaching too close, an officer could have kept him back forcefully until the victim had the assistance he needed and order was restored. The question is not whether the officers have general peace-keeping authority of that kind, but whether the officer can *arrest* Pendergrast because there is some reason to think that he has committed a robbery. In *Ellis* it is even plainer that the officers are not acting pursuant to their general peace-keeping authority. If they stop Ellis on the sidewalk and do not allow him to leave, it is because of their suspicion that he may be the daytime housebreaker.

How would you advise the officers to proceed in each case?

How would you explain your advice to (1) an observer standing on the street, (2) Pendergrast or Ellis, if he turned out to be entirely innocent?

Probable Cause

Courts have applied the test of *probable cause* in thousands of cases. Its meaning was put as well as it has ever been in a case that the Supreme Court decided a hundred years ago. An officer has probable cause for an arrest "[i]f the facts and circumstances before the officer are such as to warrant a man of prudence and caution in believing that the offence has been committed."[4] This test has two components. First, an officer making an arrest must have good reasons, ones that a reasonable person in his position would understand and accept, for believing that the person is committing or has committed a crime. Second, the reasons must be ones that the officer can communicate to another person. Sometimes an experienced officer may have a hunch that a person is "up to no good," without being able to say on what it is based. Even if he knows that similar hunches in the past have usually paid off, he does not have probable cause unless he can explain the hunch and the explanation is one that a reasonable person would accept.

If these two requirements are met, there is no restriction on the kind of information that can be used. A person's appearance or conduct may be suspicious in itself; or, as in the *Ellis* case, it may correspond to a reliable description of a criminal. Technical rules limiting the use of evidence at a trial, like the restrictions on hearsay evidence, do not apply here. Furthermore, an officer is entitled to rely on the expertise he has acquired from experience. An appearance that would be innocent to others may be suspicious to the officer; if he can explain the suspicion, it need not be ignored. If an officer gets a tip that a person has committed a crime, he can give the tip as much weight as it deserves: that is, the weight that a reasonable person with the officer's experience would give it. The more confidence he reasonably has in the source of the tip, the more he can rely on it. As long as he does not interfere with individual rights, it is proper for him to follow up his suspicions and perhaps gain additional information that adds up to probable cause for an arrest. For example, an anonymous tip would usually not give probable cause for an arrest. Even so, it might put an officer on the alert. If he watches the person in question closely and observes behavior that corroborates the tip, he may then have probable cause for an arrest.

A great many arrests do not require deliberation about the existence of probable cause. If an officer sees someone wearing a mask climb out a window late at night with a bulging pillow case over his shoulder, he does not have to ask himself whether there is probable cause for an arrest. It may turn out that the person is the homeowner who has chosen a curious time and manner of moving his possessions; but the officer's mistaken belief that he is witnessing a burglary and theft is plainly reasonable. The fact that he turns out to have been mistaken does not make his original judgment less reasonable.

There are also many cases in which it is not easy to say whether there is probable cause for an arrest. (Was there probable cause in *Pendergrast* and *Ellis*?) An officer who decides to arrest in difficult circumstances may understandably resist close examination of his decision after the fact, when the emergency is over and there is time for reflection. He may well assert that on the street the circumstances looked different from the way they look in a courtroom. Such examination is, however, essential to the preservation of constitutional values. The courts are usually aware of the stressful circumstances of an arrest and sympathetic to the officer's point of view. A conscientious officer cannot do more than apply the test of probable cause to the circumstances before him, as carefully as the situation allows. If the test is satisfied, an arrest is constitutionally valid. In the absence of probable cause, the arrest is unlawful and, as we saw in Chapter 2, evidence obtained as a direct result of the arrest is inadmissible against the person.

When Is a Person "Arrested"?

The requirement of probable cause has to be met before the arrest occurs. Otherwise, nothing that happens afterwards will make the arrest lawful. Sometimes an officer arrests someone on the street and, in the course of a search, discovers narcotics or other contraband on his person. If the arrest was made originally without probable cause, the discovery of narcotics later will not make it lawful, even though the possession of narcotics is itself a crime and furnishes probable cause for an arrest. Therefore, an officer who is trying to confirm suspicions not amounting to probable cause must not do anything in order to investigate that would itself count as an arrest. The difficulty of deciding at what moment a seizure of the person constituting an arrest has occurred is illustrated by the *Ellis* case. When in that gradually changing encounter between the officers and Ellis was he arrested?

Plainly, if an officer tells a person that he is under arrest or uses words to that effect, the requirement of probable cause has to be met. Often, however, a person is under arrest even though such words have not been used. If an officer communicates *by word or by deed* that the person is not free to go, he has made an arrest and the requirement applies. There are many uncertainties. In the *Ellis* case, was Ellis free to go when the officers summoned him to their car? If so, was he still free to go after he had answered their first questions unsatisfactorily? Most likely, the officers had not asked themselves that precise question. On the other hand, if Ellis had started to walk away, they would probably have stopped him. There is no easy way to resolve an ambiguous situation like that. Perhaps the best way to think about the problem is to ask how someone watching the scene would describe it. Even if the officer does not intend to make an arrest or has not formed any clear intention beyond the moment, if his conduct suggests that the person is no longer free to leave, an arrest has taken place.

An officer should not hesitate to observe and investigate suspicious behavior, as his duty requires. He should do so mindful of the constitutional prohibition against an arrest without probable cause and, unless he intends to arrest, should avoid conduct that would lead an ordinary person to believe that he is under constraint. In a particularly troubled situation, if it is practicable, he should make it clear that he is not making an arrest.

Sometimes an officer may conclude that there is not probable cause to arrest someone for the crime in which he is principally interested, but that the person has committed another less serious offense for which he can lawfully be arrested. The officer may anticipate that if he makes the arrest, the person will have in his possession evidence of the more serious crime or will furnish information about it. If the basis for the arrest is genuine and consistent with regular police practice, and is not a subterfuge for an arrest for the other offense, it is lawful. If it turns out that evidence of the other crime is obtained at the same time, so much the better. But an officer should not make an arrest for a technical violation of law that is ordinarily disregarded or resort to unusual tactics to circumvent the requirement of probable cause. Should that occur, a court will look beyond the surface and ignore the sham when it decides whether the arrest was made with probable cause.

Arrest on a Warrant

The second half of the Fourth Amendment refers to the issuance of "warrants...particularly describing...the persons...to be seized." In a great many situations, an arrest warrant cannot be obtained because the arresting officer has no prior knowledge or expectation that he will make an arrest. When an officer stops a crime in progress or apprehends a criminal immediately after a crime that he had no reason to anticipate, the arrest is necessarily without a warrant. In the *Pendergrast* case, for example,

United States District Court

FOR THE

_____

Magistrate's Docket No. _____

Case No. _____

UNITED STATES OF AMERICA

v

WARRANT OF ARREST

To _____[1]

You are hereby commanded to arrest _____, and bring him

here insert name of defendant or description

forthwith before the nearest available United States Magistrate to answer to a complaint charging him

with

here describe offense charged in complaint

in violation of U.S.C. Title, , Section

Date , 19 . _____,

United States Magistrate.

[1] Here insert designation of officer to whom warrant is issued.

RETURN

Received , 19 at , and executed by arrest of

at on , 19 .

_____,

Name.

_____,

Title.

Date _____ District of _____

, 19 . By _____, Deputy

FPI LC 10-75 200M 8970

32

assuming that there was probable cause for an arrest, there was no opportunity to obtain a warrant because the officer had no advance notice of the offense.

Partly because the peace-keeping efforts of the police so often require them to make an arrest without a warrant, a general rule has been established that an arrest warrant is not necessary even though there may be time to obtain one. Officers who conclude after an investigation that someone should be arrested are well-advised to obtain a warrant if that is practical. The judgment of the judicial official who issues the warrant is strong confirmation of the existence of probable cause. Courts have sometimes suggested that in a close case, a judicial determination that there was probable cause for an arrest will be made more easily if there was an arrest warrant. But, with the qualifications stated below, a warrant to arrest is not constitutionally required.

The law is clear that an arrest warrant is not necessary to arrest for a felony.* It is generally agreed also that an arrest warrant is not necessary to arrest for a misdemeanor committed in the officer's presence. In some states, the law requires that an officer obtain a warrant to arrest for a misdemeanor not committed in his presence. In those states, an officer could not arrest a person without a warrant, for example, if he had probable cause to believe that the person at some other time had committed a minor act of shoplifting that was only petty larceny. It has been suggested that the requirement of a warrant to arrest in such a case is a constitutional requirement applicable in all states. The Supreme Court has not so held, and the law must be described as uncertain in this respect. Officers should know the law of their own state and follow it. Even if state law does not require a warrant to arrest, a cautious officer will obtain a warrant before arresting for a misdemeanor not committed in his presence, if there is time to do so.

*"Felony" is the term used to characterize serious crimes. Generally, a crime is a felony if the maximum penalty for it is imprisonment for more than a year or if the place of imprisonment is the state prison or penitentiary. A misdemeanor is a less serious crime, the maximum penalty for which is imprisonment for not more than a year or the place of imprisonment for which is jail or a house of correction rather than prison. There may also be a category of very minor crimes called "petty offenses."

Figure 3-2.
Arrest Warrant

When police officers enter private premises to make an arrest, the arrest and the entry both raise questions under the Fourth Amendment. A search warrant is ordinarily necessary to enter private premises without permission (see Chapters 7, 8, and 9). An arrest warrant is sufficient for officers to enter the premises of the person named in the warrant in order to make the arrest.[5] An arrest warrant alone is not sufficient to enter premises of another person, even though officers have reason to believe that the person to be arrested can be found there; in that case, a search warrant is also necessary.[6] As discussed more fully in the chapters dealing with search and seizure, a warrant is not required if there is valid consent to the entry or an emergency makes it impracticable to delay until a warrant has been obtained.

The authority to arrest is an officer's principal source of control over a person who he believes has committed a crime. The fundamental requirement for a lawful arrest is probable cause. The importance of the issue and the difficulty of applying so general a standard to the particular facts of unplanned, ambiguous, and often tense situations result sometimes in close and debatable decisions. A fair survey of judicial decisions testing the validity of an arrest leaves no doubt that on the whole the courts have supported an officer's conscientiously exercised, professional judgment. An officer who is attentive to the constitutional principle and scrupulous in its application can be confident that his judgment will be respected.

Questions for Discussion

1. What provision of the Constitution is the source of constitutional rules affecting the law of arrest? What particular language of that provision covers arrest?

2. How is an arrest distinguished from other kinds of police action on the street?

3. From the constitutional point of view, what is an arrest?

4. Why is it important to know exactly when an arrest is made?
   How is that determined?

5. What is the basic constitutional principle limiting the authority to arrest?

6. What is probable cause for an arrest?
   On what kinds of evidence can an officer rely to establish probable cause?

7. In what circumstances is it necessary to obtain an arrest warrant before making an arrest? (With respect to misdemeanors, consult the law of your own jurisdiction.)
   In what circumstances is it advisable?

Problem Cases

The *Pendergrast* and *Ellis* cases described in this chapter illustrate how difficult it may be to decide whether, and if so when, it is appropriate to make an arrest. In *Pendergrast*, although the victim's identification of Pendergrast as one of his assailants furnished ground for suspicion, the fact that the victim was injured, drunk, and excited, and the general unlikelihood that one of the assailants would still be on the scene, make it open to question whether there was probable cause to arrest him. The court concluded that there was probable cause and that the arrest was lawful. It said that the victim's injuries corroborated his account that he had been mugged. The victim identified Pendergrast unequivocally and insisted that he was not mistaken. The circumstances, the court said, did not dilute these indications of Pendergrast's guilt "to the point of untrustworthiness": "...a showing of probable cause involves considerably less than the demonstration of guilt demands. The indicia of guilt need not be absolute, or even fully consistent; they may leave some room for doubt, and even for error."[7]

In *Ellis*, also, there was some ground for suspicion: the description of the housebreaker, Ellis's presence in the area, his entry onto the porch, and his nervousness when confronted by the officers. On the other hand, the descriptions were quite general and even conflicting, and Ellis's behavior all by itself was not very unusual or suspicious. Unless he was not arrested until after the confrontation with the officers, his nervousness during the confrontation should not be considered as an element of probable cause. One might plausibly argue that he was arrested in the constitutional sense when the officers accosted him, since he probably would not have been allowed to walk away without responding to them. In this case, a three-judge court decided, two to one, that the arrest was lawful.

The problem cases that follow present a variety of ordinary situations in which a police officer has to decide whether to make an arrest. Consider all the circumstances of the case before deciding, as appropriate, (1) whether an arrest occurred, (2) if so, when it occurred, and (3) whether, at the time of the arrest, the officer had probable cause. Consider also how the officer might have acted differently to avoid the danger of making an unlawful arrest. All of these cases are difficult. They allow you to test your understanding of probable cause and gain practice in applying your understanding to concrete facts.

1. At about 2:00 a.m., a restaurant was robbed by three men. The police broadcast a lookout containing a general description of the robbers, based on the reports of witnesses. Forty-five minutes after receiving the lookout on the radio, an officer received a call to respond to a gas station in the area in which the robbery had occurred. There a taxi driver reported that a person acting suspiciously had fled from his cab as he drove into a gas station. The officer tracked with his dog in the area for about an hour. When he returned to his cruiser, his partner told him that a man had just come out of that general area and was walking down the highway. They approached the man and arrested him at about 3:40 a.m.[8]

Was the arrest lawful?

2. At about 5:00 p.m., three men committed an assault and robbery on the street. A witness saw three men run from the scene and jump into a blue 1953 or 1954 Chevrolet hardtop. He gave officers at the scene a description of the men and the car.

Twenty minutes after the robbery, the police broadcast a lookout for three men in a 1953 blue Chevrolet, wanted in connection with the robbery. Soon afterwards, an officer stationed about four miles away saw a blue 1954 Chevrolet hardtop, occupied by four men, driving in a direction away from the scene of the crime. He broadcast his observation and the license number of the car. Headquarters broadcast a supplemental lookout containing this information. At about 5:40 p.m., two officers, who had heard both lookouts, saw the car described in the second lookout about six miles from the scene of the crime, and followed it.[9]

Do the officers have probable cause to stop the car and arrest the occupants?

3. "At 5:30 a.m....a uniformed police officer was walking his beat when he observed the defendant attempting to flag a taxicab. The defendant was carrying what appeared to be a sack and from it an electrical cord was dragging on the ground. The officer stopped the defendant, asked him where he was coming from and what his name was. The defendant replied that he was coming from a party and stated his name. Upon the request of the officer, the defendant took from his wallet a selective service card which corroborated the defendant's oral identification. The officer later testified at trial that, 'walking my beat all night long, I did not observe any party anywhere.' However, at this point, no crime had been reported to the officer and he had observed none. No warrant for the arrest of the defendant was outstanding.

"The officer then asked the defendant to accompany him to a police call box which was about one block away. When the defendant inquired whether he was under arrest, the officer replied, 'No, you are just being detained.' At the call box, the defendant seated himself on the record player contained in the sack (a pillow case) and the officer put in his call. He inquired whether there had been any reported housebreakings (up to that time he was not aware that a crime had been committed) and was told there had not been. He then requested the dispatch of a scout car to the area, when, by coincidence, a scout car appeared. At this point, the defendant fled from the scene, leaving the property behind."[10]

Had the defendant been arrested before he fled? If so, was the arrest lawful?

4. Police headquarters received an anonymous call that a man named Bernie Horowitz, described as over six feet tall and weighing more than 200 pounds and known as "Mr. Clean" because of the lack of hair on his head, was getting ready for work in the mail room of a nearby office building, and that he had in his possession a brown paper bag containing stolen savings bonds and pornographic literature. An officer went to the mail room and found a person answering the description. He identified himself as a police officer and asked the man his name. The man gave the name Bernie Horowitz. The officer then took a paper bag from him, which turned out to contain stolen bonds.[11]

Was Horowitz arrested before the discovery of the bonds? If so, was the arrest lawful?

Notes

1. The Fifth Amendment provides, with respect to the federal government: "No person shall...be deprived of life, liberty, or property, without due process of law." The Fourteenth Amendment provides that no state shall "deprive any person of life, liberty or property, without due process of law."

2. Pendergrast v. United States, 416 F.2d 776 (D.C. Cir. 1969).

3. Ellis v. United States, 264 F.2d 372, 373–74 (D.C. Cir. 1959).

4. Stacey v. Emery, 97 U.S. 642, 645 (1878). The more familiar formulation now is that officers have probable cause if "the facts and circumstances within their knowledge and of which they had reasonably trustworthy information were sufficient in themselves to warrant a man of reasonable caution in the belief that" the person to be arrested committed or was committing an offense. Carroll v. United States, 267 U.S. 132, 162 (1925).

5. Payton v. New York, 445 U.S. 573 (1980).

6. Steagald v. United States, ___ U.S. ___ (1981).

7. Pendergrast v. United States, 416 F.2d 776, 784–85 (D.C. Cir. 1969) (footnotes omitted).

8. See Gatlin v. United States, 326 F.2d 666 (D.C. Cir. 1963).

9. See Bailey v. United States, 389 F.2d 305 (D.C. Cir. 1967).

10. United States v. Mitchell, 179 F. Supp. 636, 637 (D.D.C. 1959).

11. See People v. Horowitz, 21 N.Y. 2d 55, 286 N.Y.S. 2d 473, 233 N.E. 2d 453 (1967).

THE USE OF FORCE

Most of our public officials are expected to rely on legal process rather than direct force when their authority is challenged. A police officer confronting an emergency, however, is expected to resolve it then and there, peacefully if he can but with force if necessary. Indeed, the ordinary person's reaction to an emergency that requires a forceful response is to call the police. This special aspect of the police function, their monopoly of forceful authority, carries with it special responsibility. While the community expects officers to use force when it is necessary, it also depends on them not to use force unnecessarily or in circumstances in which the consequences of its use would be worse than what it avoids.

The rules about the use of force in law enforcement vary in some respects from state to state and may be modified further by departmental regulations. There is not a uniform body of constitutional law that is largely determinative. Officers need to be fully informed about local law and how it applies to situations likely to occur. There are, however, some common general principles.

There is no preference for the use of force in police work any more than in most activities. The use of force to prevent the commission of a crime, to arrest, or to prevent escape after arrest is allowed only when there is need. If an officer can perform his work fully and effectively without force and that fact would be evident to a reasonable officer, then the use of force is not permitted. On the other hand, an officer is not expected to make close and difficult calculations of precisely how much force is needed in a tense, dangerous situation. He is authorized to use whatever force, short of deadly force, reasonably appears to be necessary for the performance of his duties. Furthermore, the performance of his duties means *safe* performance; he is not expected needlessly to risk harm to himself any more than to others.

Deadly Force

Because of the unique value of human life, the use of *deadly force* is subject to special limitations. The use of ordinary nondeadly force may result in an accidental injury or even a death. Deadly force, on the other hand, is force intended to, or likely to, cause death. The use of deadly force is generally restricted to the prevention of felonies and the apprehension of felons.* In many states, an officer is authorized to use deadly force if it reasonably appears to be necessary to prevent the commission of a

*For the distinction between felonies and misdemeanors, see p. 33 above.

felony or to arrest or prevent the escape of a person who the officer reasonably believes has committed or is committing a felony. In other states, an officer's authority to use deadly force is more limited; deadly force can be used only to prevent the commission of felonies that threaten serious personal injury, like robbery or rape, or to arrest or prevent the escape of a person whose conduct threatens such injury. Deadly force can be used also if the felon threatens to use a deadly weapon or seriously to injure the officer or another person in an effort to avoid arrest or escape from custody.

The reason for limiting the use of deadly force is that many crimes satisfy the definition of a felony but nevertheless are not a source of immediate physical danger. Despite the seriousness of these crimes, some states have concluded that in such cases, the value of life, no matter whose, should prevail over the apprehension of a criminal. If an officer is attempting to prevent the commission of a misdemeanor or to arrest or prevent the escape of a person who has committed only a misdemeanor, the use of deadly force is generally not authorized. The basis for this conclusion is once again that it is better to let a misdemeanor occur or to let the misdemeanant escape than to endanger life.

Whenever an officer uses force, he may encounter forceful resistance. If his own use of force is authorized and if the resistance threatens him with loss of life or serious injury, he can use whatever force, including deadly force, reasonably appears to be necessary to defend himself. Suppose, for example, that an officer attempts to arrest a person whom he has observed committing petty larceny, a misdemeanor. He tells the person that he is under arrest and uses no force except to take the person by the arm. If the person resists arrest and runs off, the officer can pursue him and use reasonable nondeadly force to make the arrest. But if, instead of running, the person draws a knife and threatens to stab the officer, the officer can defend himself, using even deadly force if that reasonably appears to be necessary.

Occasions when the use of force is necessary arise suddenly and unexpectedly. An officer can and should prepare for them by thinking about how to react to such situations generally. Even when the use of force is authorized, a professional police officer will avoid it as much as he can. By thinking in advance about the kind of situation he is likely to confront, a careful officer will be able to respond professionally, without needlessly endangering himself or others.

Questions for Discussion

1. What general principles apply to an officer's use of force against a person in order to effect his arrest?

2. What is deadly force?

3. What rules apply to an officer's use of deadly force in your jurisdiction?

4. If an officer uses nondeadly force to arrest a person whom he has observed committing petty larceny, and the person resists with nondeadly force, what response is the officer allowed to make?
    Suppose the person is to be arrested for a robbery?
    Suppose the person is to be arrested for petty larceny but resists and threatens to shoot the officer?

Problem Cases

In the two cases that follow, police officers used deadly force to apprehend persons whom the officers discovered committing a crime. In both cases, one of the persons was killed. Consider all the facts of the case and decide whether the use of force by the officers was an appropriate response. Consider what alternative responses were available and whether they would have been preferable. Compare these cases with cases from your own experience. By examining and contrasting factual circumstances of various cases, develop patterns of response appropriate for different types of situation.

1. "...[S]hortly after 8:00 P.M., the police radio dispatcher for the MPD's South Precinct put out a call: 'Bellevue, and Ferguson at sporting goods, prowlers inside.' Officers Calliham and Roleson in a police patrol car responded to the call and were the first to arrive on the scene, although...[officers] Cox and Richards also arrived on the scene in a patrol car almost simultaneously. SBM Co. is located at the south-east corner of South Bellevue (a street which runs in a north-south direction), a major thoroughfare, and Ferguson (an east-west street). It has a storage yard in the back (to the east) and to the northeast of the building which fronts on South Bellevue, facing west, with the main entrance being in the northwest corner of the building. The storage yard is bordered by a chain-link cyclone fence which is about 6 feet high with three strands of barbed wire on top. The fence separates the storage yard from a large drainage ditch which runs north and south at the back of the SBM Co. property, and which runs through a culvert under Ferguson Steet. There is also a similar east-west chain-link fence separating Ferguson Street from the ditch at the point where the street crosses the ditch, and a north-south chain-link fence also separates the drainage ditch on the eastern bank from the home of one Don Krag. These fences prevent access to SBM Co. or the ditch from Ferguson. From the point where it intersects with Ferguson Street, the drainage ditch runs due south for several hundred feet before curving to the west where it intersects with South Bellevue. To the east of the southern portion of the ditch, south of the Krag home, is a large housing project inhabited primarily by black families. There is a large paved area to the south of SBM Co. property along the ditch in question. This parking area is also separated from the drainage ditch by a chain-link fence, but this fence is not as high as the one surrounding SBM Co.

"When officers Calliham and Roleson arrived on the scene, they stopped their patrol car directly in front of SBM Co. which has a large glass front. Officer Calliham went to the front door and officer Roleson began running south in front of the building for the purpose of circling around behind the building at the point where the parking area adjoins the storage yard to the south. The inside of the SBM Co. was well lighted and Calliham could see three male blacks inside in the area of the soft drink machine. Richards and Cox who had also just arrived were so informed. Cox and Richards proceeded in the patrol car north and turned east on Ferguson Street along the north side of SBM Co. They stopped their car near the point where Ferguson crosses the drainage ditch. As Cox and Richards were getting out of their car, they saw two male blacks running out of the rear of the south portion of the building near the fence which separates the storage yard from the adjacent parking lot. It is approximately 54 feet from the back of the building along this east-west fence to the north-south fence along the drainage ditch. It was raining but the storage lot was lighted and the officers could see the two, who kept running and either climbed over or went under the north-south fence into the drainage ditch which was dark and obscure. Richards and/or Cox yelled for them to 'halt' repeatedly as they ran from their patrol car to the fence which separates the ditch from Ferguson Street. The two fleeing males paid no heed to the commands to stop, but instead continued running into and down the drainage ditch away from the officers.

"At this time Cox and Richards both decided to fire at the two fleeing suspects, concluding they could not apprehend them otherwise. Cox fired twice with his .38 caliber police special pistol and Richards fired three times with a shotgun loaded with buckshot. The firing was almost simultaneous. Richards did not exhaust his available shots....Richards saw one of the suspects appear to stumble upon his second or third shot. An ambulance was immediately called and a search of the ditch revealed Freddie Lee Berry lying face down a distance of some 208 feet down the ditch from where Cox and Richards had fired, and roughly 20 feet from where the youths had gone into the drainage ditch. Subsequent investigation by these officers after firing also revealed a 'stash' consisting of two shotguns and ammunition apparently taken from SBM Co. and placed in the ditch nearby where Berry was found. It is reasonable to assume Berry and his companion had not only broken in SBM Co. but had burglarized it, and were in the process of continuing the felony when interrupted. Berry had been wounded in the back of the head with a shotgun pellet and had also received a chin 'graze' from another gunshot. He was alive but unconscious at the time he was found and was taken to the hospital where he died shortly thereafter."[1]

2.   "Michael Mattis, age eighteen, and Thomas Rolf, age seventeen, were discovered in the office of a golf driving range at approximately 1:20 A.M. by police officer, Richard Schnarr. Shortly thereafter, the two boys left the office by climbing out through the back window. Schnarr shouted at the boys to halt. They ran in different directions. Schnarr then shouted, 'Halt or I'll shoot' two times. When the boys failed to stop, he fired one shot into the air and one shot at Rolf. Meanwhile, Officer Robert Marek, who had arrived on the scene, ran to intercept the boys. He collided with Mattis as he came around the corner of the building. Both fell to the pavement. Marek grabbed Mattis by the leg. Mattis broke away. Marek ran after him. Marek was losing ground. He shouted, 'Stop or I'll shoot.' Mattis did not stop. Marek, believing it necessary to take further action to prevent Mattis's escape, fired one shot in the direction of Mattis and killed him. Both officers believed that the use of their guns was reasonably necessary to effect an arrest....''[2]

Notes

1. Wiley v. Memphis Police Department, 548 F.2d 1247, 1254–55 (6th Cir. 1977) (footnotes omitted).
2. Mattis v. Schnarr, 547 F.2d 1007, 1009 (8th Cir. 1976), *vacated and remanded*, 431 U.S. 171 (1977) (*per curiam*).

CHAPTER 5

STREET INVESTIGATION

In Chapter 3, we examined constitutional limitations on the authority of a police officer to make an arrest. The principle limitation, we saw, is the requirement of probable cause to believe that the person is committing or has committed a crime. In this chapter, we shall consider what action an officer can take if he has a basis for suspicion that does not satisfy the test of probable cause.

A Brief Stop (and Frisk)

Suppose an officer on regular patrol observes someone whose behavior suggests that he may be about to commit a crime but gives the officer no ground to make an arrest. Or suppose the officer arrives at the scene of a crime and sees someone rapidly leaving the scene. The officer is free, as always, to ask for voluntary cooperation. The person leaving the scene may be entirely innocent and willing to identify himself if asked. But often, full performance of the officer's responsibilities requires more. In general, if a situation calls for prompt action and the officer takes only the action that is immediately necessary, a brief, limited interference with a person's freedom of movement is permissible. In such circumstances, the interference does not count as an arrest, and the requirement of probable cause does not apply.

The occasions when an officer may have to take swift action vary widely. Both the facts that indicate a need to act and the nature of the appropriate action have to be considered carefully. First, the need must be demonstrated by specific, articulable facts. A hunch that the

officer cannot explain may be enough for him to pay attention and to observe closely; but he is authorized to take further steps that interfere with the liberty of the person(s) whom he suspects only if he has concrete facts to go on. Second, the action that he takes must not exceed the need . While an officer cannot be expected to make a refined, subtle judgment in an unanticipated and rapidly changing course of events, he is required to act professionally, with the circumspection appropriate to the situation.

Terry v. Ohio

Police Detective McFadden was patrolling in plain clothes in downtown Cleveland during the afternoon. He had patrolled the area for thirty years. He saw two men standing together on the street. One of them walked along the street, looked in a store window, continued on past the store, and then, after pausing to look again in the same window, walked back to the other man. After they talked briefly, the second man did the same thing. Each of them in turn repeated this series of movements five or six times. While the two were together, a third man joined them and talked briefly with them, and then walked off. After about ten minutes, the two men walked off together in the direction the third man had taken. Suspecting that the three men were planning a holdup at the store, McFadden followed them and saw them stop to talk again with the third man. He approached them, identified himself as a police officer, and asked for their names. They mumbled a response. McFadden grabbed one of the men, spun him around and placed him between himself and the other two men, and frisked his outer clothing. In the end, two of the men proved to be carrying revolvers. They were arrested and subsequently prosecuted for carrying a concealed weapon.[1]

McFadden's observations did not give him probable cause to arrest the three men. He could not have said that he had reasonable grounds for belief that they were committing or had committed a crime. Even so, the frisk to determine whether they were carrying weapons was proper. Having watched them go back and forth repeatedly to look in the store window, McFadden had a basis for suspecting that they were planning a robbery. Rather than wait until—if his suspicion was correct—guns were drawn and the robbery was in progress, he had an immediate responsibility to investigate further. And since persons planning a daytime robbery would very likely be armed, there was reason for him to take the action he did. A quick frisk for weapons was permissible, although it required McFadden to interfere momentarily with the men's freedom of movement and their privacy.

The Fourth Amendment's prohibition of an unreasonable seizure of the person is fully applicable on the street, and even a brief intrusion is subject to that prohibition. A frisk, the Supreme Court said in *Terry*, "is a serious intrusion upon the sanctity of the person, which may inflict great indignity and arouse strong resentment, and it is not to be undertaken lightly."[2] The test is whether the intrusion is a reasonable response to the situation confronting the officer in the performance of his duties: whether the circumstances justify an intrusion and, if so, whether the nature and extent of the intrusion are reasonably related to the circumstances that justify it. McFadden's conduct met this test. As the Supreme Court observed, "It would have been poor police work indeed for an officer of thirty years' experience in the detection of thievery from stores in this same neighborhood to have failed to investigate this behavior further."[3] The frisk was "the tempered act of a policeman who in the course of an investigation had to make a quick decision as to how to protect himself and others from possible danger, and took limited steps to do so."[4]

The conditions in which an officer is authorized to take the kind of action taken by McFadden can be summed up as follows:

1. *The officer has a reasonable suspicion that prompt action is necessary;*

2. *The suspicion is based on specific facts that can be communicated to another person;*

3. *The situation does not permit the officer safely and responsibly to postpone action until he has learned more;*

4. The action taken is no more than the situation immediately requires; and

5. The interference with a person's liberty is not so great that, everything else aside, it counts as an arrest.

INTELLIGENCE DIVISION COPY

BOSTON POLICE DEPARTMENT
FIELD INTERROGATION and/or OBSERVATION REPORT

Check whether: Interrogated ☐ Observed ☐

Name (print)	Last	First	Initial

Address

Alias	Nickname

Location			Dist.	Date	Time

Sex	Race	Age	DOB	M or S	Soc. Sec. #	Prior Record

Hgt.	Wgt.	Comp.	Eyes	Hair	Mustache	Glasses

Scars — Deformities — Peculiarities

Describe Clothing

Car-Reg.	Make	Year	Body	Color	Oper. Lic. No.

Pass. or Driver	Occupation	Where employed or school

In company with (name & address — surname first)
1.

2.

Reasons for Interrogation or Observation

Officer Reporting	Dist./Unit	Badge No.

Figure 5–1.
*Field Interrogation
and/or Observation
Report*

Stop for Identification

The need to interfere briefly with a person's liberty arises most frequently because it is important to identify someone and ensure his subsequent availability, before there is a basis for an arrest. In a sudden street encounter, an officer may have to take steps to freeze the situation until he can find out what has happened. Usually, most of the people at the scene of a disturbance are eager or at least willing to help and will remain if an officer asks them to do so. If they are not willing, in some circumstances the officer can require them to remain just the same.

An officer has no general authority to require a person in public to identify himself or give an account of what he is doing. In this country, there is no general duty to carry personal identification. A request for identification may be the most appropriate measure for a police officer to take; but ordinarily a person need not comply with the request. A refusal to comply may, along with other facts, have a bearing on the officer's next action. By itself, it does not authorize an arrest or detention against the person's will. In order to stop a person and require him to identify himself, an officer must have "a reasonable suspicion, based on objective facts, that the individual is involved in criminal activity."[5]

> Two officers respond to the scene of a mugging in the early evening. The victim has been knocked to the ground and her pocketbook has been taken. She is not badly injured but she is upset. She describes her assailant as a young man about six feet tall and wearing a green sweater. There are few people in the area, and there are no witnesses to the mugging. One of the officers remains with the victim while the other looks around. About two blocks away, he sees a man of average height wearing a dark blue sweater walking rapidly in a direction away from the scene of the crime.

What should the officer do?

> The officer hails the man in the blue sweater. The man looks up, sees the officer, and continues to walk away, more rapidly than before.

What should the officer do?

The officer pursues the man and directs him to stop. He stops in front of a row of stores, most of which are closed. The street is lit by street lamps. As the officer approaches the man, he does nothing but wait.

What should the officer do?

The officer says to the man, "Give me your name, please, and tell me what you are doing here." The man mumbles an unintelligible response and starts to walk away.

What should the officer do?

Knowing that a mugging has just occurred nearby and that the man whom he encounters matches the description of the mugger, the officer has a reasonable suspicion, based on specific facts, that the man has committed a serious crime. In view of the generality of the description, however, and without an identification by the victim or other evidence, he lacks probable cause for an arrest. Yet, unless he takes action immediately, the man will probably disappear for good.

In those circumstances, the officer's decision to hail the man is easily justified. When the man responds by disregarding the officer and increasing his speed, a further step is reasonable. Having been stopped, his refusal to identify himself furnishes additional ground for suspicion; but without more, there is not probable cause for his arrest. In view of the seriousness of the crime and the inability to trace the man if he should now disappear, the officer can require him to return briefly to the scene of the crime to see whether the victim can identify him. Furthermore, the nature of the crime justifies a frisk for the officer's safety. Had the man's response been different, had he furnished apparently reliable identification and given an innocent explanation for his presence on the street, the same action might not be authorized.

Brown v. Texas

"At 12:45 in the afternoon...Officers Venegas and Sotelo of the El Paso Police Department were cruising in a patrol car. They observed appellant [Brown] and another man walking in opposite directions away from one another in an alley. Although the two men were a few feet apart when they first were seen....both officers believed the two had been together or were about to meet until the patrol car appeared.

"The car entered the alley, and Officer Venegas got out and asked appellant to identify himself and explain what he was doing there. The other man was not questioned or detained. The officer testified that he stopped appellant because the situation 'looked suspicious and we had never seen that subject in that area before.' The area of El Paso where appellant was stopped has a high incidence of drug traffic. However, the officers did not claim to suspect appellant of any specific misconduct, nor did they have any reason to believe that he was armed.

"Appellant refused to identify himself and angrily asserted that the officers had no right to stop him. Officer Venegas replied that he was in a 'high drug problem area'; officer Sotelo then 'frisked' appellant, but found nothing."[6] Brown was arrested for violation of a state statute requiring a person who is lawfully stopped by a police officer to give his name and address on request.

The officers who stopped Brown had only a general suspicion. The specific facts known to them did not indicate criminal misconduct; they had not observed anything that distinguished Brown from other pedestrians in the area. Therefore, the usual rule that a person does not have to identify himself applied. While it was perhaps good work to assert a police presence in the area, the officers could not take the further step of forcibly interfering with Brown's liberty, even briefly. Since the stop of Brown was not lawful, his conviction under the state statute was invalid.

Ordinarily, then, a stop for identification should be made only if there is a well-founded suspicion that the person is presently engaged in criminal activity or was recently engaged in criminal activity that is now being investigated. In other circumstances an officer can only request information without indicating that the person is required to respond or detaining him if he does not.

Unlawful Investigative Detention

Dunaway v. New York

"On March 26...the proprietor of a pizza parlor in Rochester, N.Y., was killed during an attempted robbery. On August 10...Detective Anthony Fantigrossi of the Rochester Police was told by another officer that an informant had supplied a possible lead implicating petitioner [Dunaway] in the crime. Fantigrossi questioned the supposed source of the lead—a jail inmate awaiting trial for burglary—but learned nothing that supplied 'enough information to get a warrant' for petitioner's arrest.... Nevertheless, Fantigrossi ordered other detectives to 'pick up' petitioner and 'bring him in.'... Three detectives located petitioner at a neighbor's house on the morning of August 11. Petitioner was taken into custody; although he was not told he was under arrest, he would have been physically restrained if he had attempted to leave.... He was driven to police headquarters in a police car and placed in an interrogation room, where he was questioned by officers after being given the warnings required by Miranda v. Arizona[*].... Petitioner waived counsel and eventually made statements and drew sketches that incriminated him in the crime."[7]

Even though the officers did not tell Dunaway that he was under arrest and did not book him, he had in effect been arrested. The intrusion on Dunaway's liberty was too much like an arrest to be treated as a brief detention authorized without probable cause. Although the informer's tip led Detective Fantigrossi to suspect that Dunaway was involved in the killing and the detective had a legitimate interest in investigating the tip, the Fourth Amendment requires that an arrest be made only

[*] See pp. 166–168 below.

on probable cause. That constitutional requirement cannot be avoided when probable cause is lacking simply by calling an arrest by another name. Dunaway's prolonged investigative detention was in reality an unlawful arrest.

When all the conditions for a lawful investigative stop are listed, it may appear that they restrict an officer's responses too much. In fact, the conditions give an officer authority to take action that reasonably appears to be necessary, but no more than is necessary. We depend on the professional competence and good judgment of the officer to strike the balance between the goals of a lawful, orderly, and safe community on the one hand and individual freedom on the other. If officers were allowed to stop and question a person at any time, on any suspicion, no doubt more crimes would be cleared and some would be prevented; but the cost in freedom would be great. If they were never authorized to stop a person even briefly, without probable cause for an arrest, there might be some gain in liberty, but we should have lost significant capacity to control crime.

Questions for Discussion

1. In what circumstances can an officer stop a person whom he suspects of involvement in a crime, without having probable cause for an arrest?
What restrictions apply to such a stop?

2. In what circumstances can an officer frisk a person whom he stops, without having probable cause for an arrest?

3. When can a person who is not under arrest be required to identify himself?

4. Can an officer who lawfully stops a person without having probable cause for an arrest require the person to accompany him elsewhere?
If so, in what circumstances and for what purposes?
Can he require the person to accompany him to the police station for questioning?

Problem Cases

In the first case that follows, consider what action the officer ought to take initially and how he ought to react to various possible responses of the man in question. In the remaining cases, consider whether the actions that the officer took were lawful. Consider the basis for the action and whether the action was reasonably related to the circumstances. Consider also whether the officer might have followed some other procedure that would have been preferable.

1. Two men held up a grocery store at about 10:00 p.m. An officer on patrol in that area responded to the scene and was told by other officers that one of the robbers, who had carried a gun, was a tall man of large build, with dark hair, and wearing a red jacket. Twenty minutes later, about six blocks from the store, the officer saw a tall man with dark hair and wearing a red sweater emerge from a bar. The man was carrying a small, zippered satchel.

What should the officer do?

2. "...New York City Policeman Saverio Alesi was patrolling in uniform on Eighth Avenue between 42nd and 45th Streets. At approximately 3:00 P.M. he observed...Magda talking with another man on the north side of 43rd Street just west of Eighth Avenue. They were about thirty to thirty-five feet from Alesi, who was standing on the southwest corner of the intersection.

"As Alesi watched the two men, he saw them exchange something. Although he could not see exactly what had changed hands, he did see that each man gave and received something simultaneously. After the exchange, the unidentified participant looked in the officer's direction. Immediately after doing so, he turned away in a 'rapid motion' and proceeded west on 43rd Street. Meanwhile, Madga crossed 43rd Street at an angle and started down Eighth Avenue toward 42nd Street. As he passed, Alesi tapped him on the shoulder and asked him to stop. Magda turned to face Alesi and slowed his pace but continued down Eighth Avenue, walking backwards. The two men proceeded in this fashion for several steps, covering about ten feet before they both stopped.

"Alesi inquired about what had taken place on 43rd Street, and at first Magda said that nothing had happened. When asked a second time, Magda replied, 'All right. I bought a marijuana cigarette for a dollar,' and produced the cigarette from his inside coat pocket. Alesi placed him under arrest and walked him back to 43rd Street in a vain attempt to find the other man. Alesi then searched Magda and, upon discovering an unloaded handgun and a robbery demand note, took him to the police station and booked him on gun and drug charges."[8] Alesi knew that there was narcotics activity in the area in which he first observed Magda.

3.   "The detective, Richard Delaney...testified that on the day of the arrest he received an anonymous telephone call at the police station informing him that 'there was a male, white youth on the corner of 135th and Jamaica Avenue...[who] had a loaded 32 calibre revolver in his left hand jacket pocket.' The caller also stated that the youth was 'eighteen', had 'blue eyes, blond hair' and was wearing 'white chino-type pants.'

"Delaney then proceeded to that location and observed from across the street an individual who 'matched perfectly' the description given to Delaney by the informer. The youth...'was standing in the middle of a group of children that had just finished bowling.' Thereupon, Delaney crossed the street, 'took him...by the arm and put him against the wall and took the revolver out of his left-hand jacket pocket.' Delaney did not notice any bulge in the...pocket prior to the search as the weapon 'was inside the lining of the jacket.'

"...Delaney...had never before arrested...[the youth] and...had never seen him in the neighborhood."[9]

4.   "...About 2:50 A.M....Sergeant Bergin, while in the vicinity of Commonwealth Avenue, Brookline, observed the defendant walking on Crowninshield Road to Commonwealth Avenue. There had been several breaking and entering incidents in the neighborhood, but none had been reported that night. The officer stopped the defendant and inquired about his identity and purpose for being abroad. The defendant identified himself and stated that he was walking from Boston to visit a friend who lived on Commonwealth Avenue in Brookline. When

questioned as to the route he was taking, the
defendant replied that 'he had felt like taking a walk.'
Observing that the defendant was carrying a paper bag
with the name of 'Mal's Department Store' on the
outside, the officer asked if he might examine its
contents, and the defendant readily assented. The bag
contained new articles of clothing, consisting of
underwear and socks, and a sales slip bearing the date
of June 28. The defendant informed the officer that he
had purchased the articles on the preceding day, July
1. Because the items of clothing were apparently not
of the defendant's size, the officer became suspicious
and frisked him to determine if he was carrying any
weapons. The frisk consisted of the officer quickly
running his hands over the defendant's clothing. He
discovered, in the small of the defendant's back and
tucked under his shirt and belt, a screwdriver, the
shaft of which was seven inches long; it was not new
and had paint marks on both the shaft and handle.
The defendant said he had bought the screwdriver
along with the clothing at Mal's Department Store.
The defendant was thereupon arrested and taken to
the police station where a thorough search was made.
He was charged with possession of burglarious
instruments."[10]

5. "...In the early morning hours (approximately 1:15
A.M.)...William Sadler, a tractor driver employed by
REA, had exited from the REA terminal located at
42nd Street and 11th Avenue in Manhattan and
stopped for a traffic light close by. At that time, Sadler observed a man, later identified as Lewis, walking
directly in front of his tractor carrying a brown carton
which looked like it came from REA. After the light
changed, Sadler sought out the police and reported
his observation to New York City Patrolmen Murphy
and Connor who were in the vicinity. He proceeded
with them in their radio car to locate the individual
he had just observed.

"When stopped by the police and queried on the
street, Lewis explained that he had found the carton a
short distance away under an overhang between 10th
and 11th Avenues on 41st Street. He stated that he
had inquired of an old woman standing next to the
carton whether it belonged to her and upon her negative reply, he decided to take it. In response to
inquiries concerning Lewis' presence in the vicinity of
the terminal, Lewis claimed that he was employed by

the Circle Line at 42nd Street and 12th Avenue as a deck swabber, and had just finished his work for the night. When the police, however, indicated that they intended to verify this statement, Lewis admitted that he did not work for the Circle Line.

"During these few moments of street inquiry, Lewis placed the carton on the hood of a parked car. Murphy then was able to observe that the package had been opened and the seals and labels removed. In addition, he noticed an imprinted stamp bearing the words 'REA' and 'Atlanta, Georgia.' Sadler, at the policeman's request, examined the package and confirmed that REA utilized such a stamp for the purpose of indicating the source of shipments. Lewis was then taken into custody....Patrolmen Murphy and Connor were veteran policemen seasoned in the neighborhood and familiar with the frequency of similar criminal occurrences."[11]

6. "...[A]bout 11:15 A.M., two detectives in plain clothes assigned to the narcotics squad of the Metropolitan Police Department were engaged in the investigation of narcotic activities. Slowly cruising in an unmarked car in the vicinity of North Capitol and R. Streets, N.W. in the District of Columbia, they overtook and drove abreast of two men, walking ahead of them on R Street. They thereupon immediately identified one as John Arthur 'Jap' Palmer, a known narcotic addict, but did not know the other...[Green]. The officers stopped the car, addressed Palmer by name, and called the two men over to them....

"Palmer heeded their call and started toward the car. Green, however, 'took off'...and ran into a nearby yard. He passed the occupant of a house as she sat on a bench near her front steps. He ran up the steps, across the landing at the top, and tried to open her front door. She called out 'Fellow, what do you want? I live in there,' but received no answer. Officer Brewer started after...[Green]. The woman then said, 'You all take him in the street.'"[12] Green was arrested for attempted unlawful entry. He was searched and narcotics were found on his person.

7. "...Patrolman John DeRosa, a narcotics investigator assigned to the New York Joint Task Force, had under surveillance the La Concha restaurant on Manhattan's Upper West Side. The restaurant was known to the police to be a meeting place for persons engaged in

narcotics activities. Accompanying DeRosa in a government car was Detective Patrick Campbell of the New York City Police Department.

"Late in the evening, the officers saw Santana and a companion, who later turned out to be Alfredo Aviles, drive up to the restaurant and illegally double park in front. Santana and Aviles entered the restaurant and returned to the car half an hour later, with Santana carrying a brown paper bag. DeRosa testified that he recognized Santana as being among the 100 major narcotics violators in New York City, according to police files, and that an anonymous informant had told him Santana was 'heavily engaged in narcotic activities.' Santana and his companion then drove to a nearby apartment building at 331 West End Avenue, with the police following in their vehicle. After again double-parking the car, Santana entered the building and emerged about ten minutes later carrying a second brown paper bag.

"Meanwhile the officers left their vehicle and continued the surveillance on foot. Santana reentered his car on the driver's side and prepared to drive off. DeRosa then walked up to the car and tapped at the window on Santana's side. When Santana lowered the window, DeRosa asked him to produce his driver's license and registration. Santana voluntarily opened the door, stepped out of the car, and reached for his wallet, leaving the door about two feet open. DeRosa then pushed the door the rest of the way open—about another foot—and stepped between the door and the car. He testified that from that position he could see a clear plastic bag filled with a white powdery substance that had been secreted between the door and the front seat. DeRosa seized the bag, which he correctly assumed to contain narcotics, and the officers immediately arrested Santana and Aviles for drug violations."[13] The first brown paper bag proved to contain food and the second bag a can of frozen orange juice.

8. "At 12:15 a.m....Kenneth Steck, a police officer assigned to the Tactical Patrol Force of the New York Police Department, was working the 6:00 p.m. to 2:00 a.m. tour of duty, assigned to patrol by foot a certain section of Brooklyn. While walking his beat on a street illuminated by ordinary street lamps and devoid of pedestrian traffic, he and his partner noticed someone walking on the same side of the street in their

direction. When the solitary figure...Louis De Bour, was within 30 or 40 feet of the uniformed officers, he crossed the street. The two policemen followed suit and when De Bour reached them Officer Steck inquired as to what he was doing in the neighborhood. De Bour, clearly but nervously, answered that he had just parked his car and was going to a friend's house.

"The patrolman then asked De Bour for identification. As he was answering that he had none, Officer Steck noticed a slight waist-high bulge in defendant's jacket. At this point the policeman asked De Bour to unzipper his coat. When De Bour complied with this request Officer Steck observed a revolver protruding from his waistband. The loaded weapon was removed from behind his waistband and he was arrested for possession of the gun.

"...[T]he encounter lasted 'a few minutes'....Officer Steck...believed [De Bour] might have been involved with narcotics and crossed the street to avoid apprehension."[14]

Notes

1. Terry v. Ohio, 392 U.S. 1 (1968).

2. *Id.* at 17 (footnote omitted).

3. *Id.* at 23.

4. *Id.* at 28.

5. Brown v. Texas, 443 U.S. 47, 51 (1979).

6. *Id.* at 48–49.

7. Dunaway v. New York, 442 U.S. 200, 202–203 (1979) (footnotes omitted).

8. United States v. Magda, 547 F.2d 756, 757–58 (2d Cir. 1976) (footnotes omitted).

9. People v. Taggart, 20 N.Y. 2d 335, 337–38, 283 N.Y.S. 2d 1, 4, 229 N.E. 2d 581, 582–83 (1967).

10. Commonwealth v. Matthews, 355 Mass. 378, 378–79, 244 N.E. 2d 908, 909 (1969).

11. United States v. Lewis, 362 F.2d 759, 760–61 (2d Cir. 1966).

12. Green v. United States, 259 F.2d 180, 181–82 (D.C. Cir. 1958) (footnote omitted).

13. United States v. Santana, 485 F.2d 365, 366–67 (2d Cir. 1973) (footnotes omitted).

14. People v. De Bour, 40 N.Y. 2d 210, 213–14, 386 N.Y.S. 2d 375, 378, 352 N.E. 2d 562, 565 (1976).

CHAPTER 6

ROADBLOCKS AND VEHICLE STOPS

The constant use of automobiles for public and private purposes affects the work of the police as it affects all aspects of American life. Automobiles have dramatically increased the mobility of the police and thereby their ability to preserve order over a wide area and to respond to the scene of a crime. Automobiles have also increased the mobility of criminals, who move quickly to or from the scene of a crime, travel long distances to escape detection and avoid capture, and transport the fruits of a crime or contraband without difficulty. Law enforcement personnel have had to adapt their techniques to the increased capacities of criminals without disrupting the lives of law-abiding persons, who use automobiles for the widest variety of ordinary activities.

Constitutional law has sought an accommodation between the right of people to conduct their affairs in private when they use an automobile and the special problems of law enforcement when an automobile is used by criminals. The main principles are derived from the Fourth Amendment. In this chapter, we shall apply them generally to motor vehicles. In Chapter 7, we shall consider special rules about searches of vehicles, also derived from the Fourth Amendment.

Most of the references in this chapter are to automobiles. The discussion applies equally to any kind of vehicle that shares the characteristics of mobility, speed, and use on public ways. Cases involving an airplane or a motorboat occasionally arise; the relevant principles are the same. Sometimes it is not altogether clear whether a movable living unit should be treated as a motor vehicle or a residence. Such units vary from the truck with a small, temporarily attached camping cap, to large, multiroomed mobile homes, which are moved infrequently from one permanent location to another. While the extreme examples are easily classified, others may not be. An officer cannot do more than rely on his good sense. Insofar as a mobile living unit shares the characteristics of

ordinary vehicles and those characteristics are relevant in the circumstances, it should be treated as a vehicle. If the unit is used as living quarters, it should be treated as such, despite the possibility that it might at some time be moved.

General Regulation and Investigative Stops

We are all used to the fact that the use of an automobile is subject to regulation as other private movement is not. The power of an automobile and the danger of its use without adequate care and safeguards make it in everyone's interest that there be licensing requirements for drivers and registration and safety inspection of cars. Extensive and elaborate traffic codes are observed by the vast majority of drivers and enforced seriously. Regulation is so familiar that we scarcely notice it.

Most of the regulation has little to do with crime. Even traffic violations, for which a great many persons get "tickets" at one time or another, are regarded as noncriminal; the violator pays his fine by mail and thinks no more about it. Just the same, traffic control and the enforcement of other automotive regulations, like safety inspections and parking restrictions, are a responsibility of the police. Within any large police department, the administrative separation between routine traffic assignments and criminal investigation is clear. To ordinary persons it is more likely simply to be "the police" who do both kinds of work. The law requires us to distinguish carefully between the authority of the police that grows out of routine traffic and automotive regulation on the one hand, and their authority to investigate crime on the other. Usually, that distinction presents no difficulty. When a routine traffic measure turns up evidence of a crime or when police rely on a routine measure to carry out an investigative function, the matter is more complicated.

Two general principles reflect the distinction just described:

1. Ordinary traffic regulation and enforcement of licensing, registration, inspection, and similar regulative measures are lawful, provided that they are applied generally and carried out on a routine basis, without singling out a particular person or automobile for special attention. It is permissible, for

example, to enforce licensing or registration regulations by random checks according to a set pattern, like every tenth car, or to enforce safety requirements by a check of all cars that do not display a current inspection sticker. However, officers may not depart from a pattern of random enforcement or, in the absence of such a pattern, stop a particular automobile for traffic control in order to carry out an investigative purpose.

2. An investigative stop or an arrest of a driver or passenger in a vehicle is authorized on the same basis as a stop or arrest of a person on the street. In Chapter 3, we discussed the requirement of probable cause for an arrest. Having probable cause, an officer can halt a car to arrest someone inside. Similarly, if the requirements for an investigative stop are satisfied, an officer can halt a car long enough to accomplish the purpose of the stop. As we saw in Chapter 5, one of the requirements for a stop when there is not probable cause for an arrest is a need for prompt action. In estimating that factor, an officer can properly take the mobility of an automobile into account.

Self-Protection

We saw earlier that an officer investigating likely criminal activity on the street is allowed to make a protective frisk if he has a basis for believing that the persons involved may be armed. The reason for allowing the frisk is simply that an officer cannot be expected to undertake a potentially dangerous task without being given authority that enables him to avoid the danger. The same reasoning applies to the stop of a vehicle. The Supreme Court has recognized the danger to an officer who brings an unidentified motorist to a halt. Having a valid ground for the stop, the officer does not need a separate, additional basis of suspicion to order the driver to get out of the car.[1] That limited protective measure is a minimal intrusion on liberty and can always be taken. The law is not entirely clear whether passengers can also routinely be ordered to get out of the car. An officer should not needlessly order passengers to alight during an ordinary stop for a traffic offense. If the circumstances furnish a specific reason for taking extra precautions, such an order will be upheld. Once the occupants are out of the car, a protective frisk of their persons is proper only if there is the basis for it described in Chapter 5.

Limitations

Abuse of the authority to stop a vehicle occurs most frequently because an officer uses his responsibility for traffic control as an excuse for investigation. An officer is not prevented from reacting to indications of criminal activity that he discovers in the course of routine traffic regulation. For example, if he stops a car for a traffic violation and without any special effort on his part sees evidence of a crime on the front seat, he may then have probable cause for an arrest. But traffic regulation is not a means of criminal investigation and cannot be used to justify a stop for investigative purposes. Furthermore, none of the rules considered in this chapter authorizes a search of a vehicle or its occupants (beyond a protective frisk, if that is appropriate). An officer who stops a vehicle for a regulatory purpose should not take any special action simply because it gives him an opportunity to examine the interior. Although it may appear difficult to keep the regulatory and investigative functions separate after a car has been lawfully stopped, careful adherence to the two principles discussed above will allow the separation to be made. Doing so, officers preserve the constitutional balance between private use of motor vehicles and the needs of law enforcement.

Questions for Discussion

1. How are traffic and automotive regulation distinguished from criminal investigation?

2. What methods can be used to carry out routine traffic and regulatory measures on the highway?

3. When is an officer authorized to stop a car on the highway for criminal investigation?

Problem Cases

In the following cases, consider the nature of the actions taken and whether they were authorized. If they were authorized, explain on what basis.

1. On December 31, between 11:00 p.m. and 1:00 a.m., a highway patrol stopped all cars entering the highway at designated intersections for a license and registration check.

2. Observing that the driver of a car appeared to be younger than the minimum age at which a license could be obtained, an officer stopped it and asked the driver for his license and the registration. The officer had observed no violation of the traffic laws.

3. At 2:00 a.m., officers on highway patrol saw a black car with brightly painted red stripes running along both sides and ending in a design representing an eagle along the hood and front fenders. After following the car for about five miles and observing no violation of the traffic laws, they stopped it. Approaching the driver's side, one of the officers directed the driver to alight. The other officer shined a flashlight into the car from the other side, to see whether there was anyone in the rear seat. He saw what appeared to be the handle of a shotgun on the floor in the rear. The driver was asked for his license and the registration. At the same time, the second officer opened the passenger door and retrieved a shotgun from under the front seat. He felt around under the seat and withdrew a paper bag, which proved to contain narcotics. The driver was then placed under arrest.

4. Two police officers on highway patrol duty noticed an old, battered car going in the opposite direction. The driver and a passenger in the front seat were young men whose appearance was unkempt. Immediately after passing the police car, the other car turned off the highway onto a side road. The officers crossed the highway and followed the car. After two miles, the car turned back onto the highway and continued in the same direction. A few miles farther on, not having observed any traffic violation, the officers stopped the car. Both occupants got out and walked over to the police car. While one of the officers asked the driver for his license and the registration, the other walked over to the car and reached into the open window on the driver's side to test the horn and lights. As he did so, he saw a plastic bag containing a substance that looked like marijuana protruding from under the seat. He opened the car and removed the bag.

5. The police had information that a meeting of leaders of organized crime would take place at a house in the country. The house was near the end of a little-traveled public road. On the weekend on which the meeting was to take place, the police set up a roadblock several miles from the house. All cars approaching the roadblock were directed to stop. The drivers were required to show a license and registration and were then allowed to proceed.

6. Police officers had Cavallino under surveillance as a suspect in bank robberies. Having reason to believe that he was about "to depart," they were instructed

by their superior, who was "aware of Cavallino's propensity to violate motor vehicle laws," to follow him and arrest him if he violated any law. They stopped him when he "substantially exceeded the speed limit." He refused to produce his license. The officers arrested him for both offenses, misdemeanors under state law.[2]

Notes

1. Pennsylvania v. Mimms, 434 U.S. 106 (1977) (*per curiam*).
2. United States v. Cavallino, 498 F.2d 1200, 1201 (5th Cir. 1974).

CHAPTER 7

SEARCH AND SEIZURE: WITHOUT A SEARCH WARRANT

Few topics in constitutional law have generated as much discussion as the law of search and seizure. The basic constitutional text is the Fourth Amendment, which we have already considered in connection with arrest:

> *The right of the people to be secure in their persons, houses, papers, and effects, against unreasonable searches and seizures, shall not be violated, and no warrants shall issue, but upon probable cause, supported by oath or affirmation, and particularly describing the place to be searched, and the persons or things to be seized.*

Interpretation of that brief text and its application to concrete problems have been a constant source of debate and disagreement in the Supreme Court and lower federal and state courts. Even among themselves, the Justices of the Supreme Court have often disagreed about a general approach or the result in particular cases. Small wonder, then, that officers acting in the heat and haste of law enforcement have difficulty knowing what the Constitution allows.

Despite the confusion, there are a small number of general constitutional principles. An officer cannot do more than learn them and apply them conscientiously to the changing situations that he confronts. If he does, it will happen rarely that a court later finds his action to have been unlawful. A visible and consistent pattern of conscientious adherence to constitutional principles will itself help to sustain the conclusion that the law was not violated in a particular case.

Some recurrent police situations so often present circumstances in which a search is reasonable that a general rule authorizes a search without a search warrant or a specific justification in each case. In this chapter, we shall consider the law pertaining to searches of this kind, which occur in the course of regular peace-keeping and investigative assignments. The two chapters that follow continue the discussion of search and seizure in other circumstances.

Search and Seizure

One reason why there has been so much confusion in this area of constitutional law is that the phrase *search and seizure* is applied without differentiation to a number of dissimilar police actions. An officer's search of an unknown person whom he has arrested on the street and a planned search of premises pursuant to a search warrant are both searches for constitutional purposes; but from the functional perspective of an officer the two operations are considerably different. Similarly, a search of a house in pursuit of a criminal thought to be hiding there and a search of a house for evidence of a crime may have little in common for the officers, even though the authority to conduct both is subject to the requirements of the Fourth Amendment. The common feature of police actions characterized constitutionally as a search is simply that they involve an intrusion on the kind of personal privacy that the Amendment protects.

As a general matter, any official entrance into or inspection of a place—as large as a house or as small as a wallet—that a person ordinarily can keep private is a search, an invasion of privacy for which justification is required. An officer can freely observe the activities of people on the street because he is not observing anything that a person has a right to keep private in those circumstances. But he cannot enter a private house to observe the same activities without a justification consistent with the rights protected by the Fourth Amendment. Even though the activities observed in the two cases might be the same, the entrance into private premises in the latter case brings the Amendment into play. As we shall consider more fully below, provided that a search is lawful and officers are rightfully present where and when the search occurs, they can seize any item that is evidence of a crime.

Search Incident to an Arrest

We have already noticed circumstances in which an officer is authorized to take an action because it is necessary for the safe, effective performance of another lawful function. If an officer has a duty to perform in the presence of a person whom he reasonably believes to be armed and dangerous, he is authorized to perform a frisk for his own protection, even though without that special justification the frisk would be a plain violation of the

Fourth Amendment. The same reasoning applies when an officer makes an arrest. Most people who are arrested submit peaceably and carry no weapon. But the arresting officer cannot rely on that generality. For his own safety and perhaps the safety of others, he needs assurance that the person will not use a weapon to attack him or to escape.

The well-established rule is that when an officer makes a lawful arrest, a search *incident to the arrest* is also lawful. The Supreme Court has expressed three reasons why a search is allowed to accompany an arrest: (1) to avoid danger to the officer and others, (2) to prevent an escape, and (3) to prevent the destruction of evidence. These reasons are sufficient to justify a search of the arrested person and the area immediately around him and within his control[1]

Unlike situations in which a particular justification is required—for example, the specific indications of danger without which a frisk is not authorized—particular justification is not required for a search incident to an arrest. A search after an arrest is so often necessary that an officer is allowed to make an incident search without weighing the particular circumstances of each arrest. The rule authorizes a search only incident to an actual lawful arrest, however. If an arrest is made without probable cause, it is constitutionally unlawful, and a search incident to the arrest is likewise unlawful.

The search of an arrested person can include a search of his clothing as well as of the ordinary small things that he carries in his pockets, like a wallet. Similarly, a woman's handbag can be searched. A line has to be drawn between such things "immediately associated with the person,"[2] which can be searched incident to an arrest, and other, larger containers in the person's possession at the time of an arrest. In general, a container can be searched if it would probably be described not simply as carried by the arrested person but as carried "on his person." If a container is small and of a kind that people ordinarily use to carry things about wherever one goes, it is more likely to be treated as an extension of the person and subject to an incident search; if it is very large or is something being used as a container for a particular purpose, it is less likely to be regarded as carried on the person. A cautious officer will not search, as an incident of an arrest, containers other than those carried in a pocket of the person's clothing or a woman's handbag.

United States v. Chadwick

Federal narcotics agents had reason to believe that a trunk containing narcotics was being transported by train from San Diego to Boston. When the train arrived in Boston, agents observed the trunk being unloaded and were able to confirm their suspicion. They watched three persons move the trunk to a waiting car and arrested them when they were lifting it into the car. Having taken custody of the trunk, which was locked, the agents opened it and searched it at headquarters an hour and a half after the arrests.[3]

The Supreme Court said that the search was unlawful and that the narcotics found in the trunk could not be used in evidence. The trunk was not on the person of the arrested men, and its search was not incident to their arrest. Having probable cause to believe that it contained narcotics, the agents should have retained it in their custody and promptly obtained a warrant to search it.

A search beyond things in the arrested person's immediate possession is narrowly limited. Officers are not permitted to search an entire house or apartment simply because they have arrested an occupant within. Having arrested a person in one room, a search of other rooms is not necessary to carry out the arrest effectively and, therefore, cannot be justified as an incident of the arrest. A good rule of thumb is that a search incident to an arrest can extend no further than a small area around the person, say within his arm's reach or a step or two. That much is usually assumed to be an area within his control, even if in the actual circumstances he is unlikely to grab anything. If a person were sitting at his desk when officers entered to arrest him, they would be able to look briefly through items lying immediately in view on top of the desk; but a lengthy and meticulous examination of many papers or a thorough search of the desk drawers would exceed what the rule allows.

In order to determine whether a search beyond the person arrested was proper, a court is likely to ask:

1. Was the person under restraint, such as handcuffs, before the search was made?

2. Was the place searched one from which the person could easily have grabbed something? An officer has less reason to open and search a locked desk drawer, for example, than an unlocked and partly open drawer.

3. Did the arresting officers far outnumber the person(s) arrested?

4. What were the positions of the officer(s) and the arrested person(s) relative to the place searched?

Such questions help the court to decide whether the search was reasonably necessary to accomplish the arrest and was an incident of it rather than an independent search.

While the cases involving a search incident to an arrest may appear to make fine and sometimes arbitrary distinctions, the applicable rules can be simply stated:

1. *A search of the person arrested, things carried "on his person," and a small area around him and within his immediate control is permissible.*

2. *Any search that reasonably appears to be necessary to protect the officer or others from an attack by the person arrested, to prevent his escape, or to prevent him from destroying evidence is permissible.*

3. *A search beyond the limits specified in (1) and (2) is not incident to the arrest and cannot be justified on that basis.*

Search Incident to Arrest—The Occupant of an Automobile. In a case decided in 1981,[4] the Supreme Court recognized that the general rule covering searches incident to an arrest might be especially hard to apply when the driver or occupant of an automobile is arrested. In some cases, the arresting officer may have reason to fear that the person will grab a weapon or destructible evidence from almost anywhere in the passenger area; the whole area is sufficiently within his control to be included in a search incident to his arrest. Concluding that this is generally, if not invariably, so and that a uniform workable rule is desirable, the Court held that whenever a custodial arrest is made of the occupant of an automobile, a search incident to the arrest can extend to the entire passenger area, including all containers, closed or open, within it. The arresting officer(s) can open and search the glove compartment or similar receptacles attached to the car, as well as luggage, boxes, paper bags, clothing, or other containers anywhere in the passenger area. The authority to search is general and does not depend on the particular circumstances. So long as the search occurs at substantially the same time and place as the arrest, it can be made after the arrested person has left the automobile. The same rule, of course, covers trucks and vehicles of all kinds that share the relevant characteristics of automobiles.

While this rule gives an arresting officer broad authority to search, two limitations should be noted. First, the rule covers only the passenger area and does not authorize a search of the trunk or under the hood or elsewhere. Even within the passenger area, a search should not be so intensive or unusual that it includes places which would never be immediately accessible; the rule would not, for example, authorize removal of a seat in the passenger area in order to search an otherwise inaccessible area behind it. Second, the rule applies only to a *custodial* arrest. Often, an officer stops a driver for a traffic offense and gives him a ticket, but does not take him into custody. In that situation, the officer should not search the driver, unless particular circumstances justify a protective frisk, and should not search the automobile. Nor should an officer make a custodial arrest simply in order to search if the usual practice is to give a ticket. Unless a custodial arrest is not unusual in the circumstances, a search is not likely to be upheld as an incident of it. The search is allowed in these cases because the arrest followed by custody makes it necessary; that reasoning cannot be reversed, so that the arrest is merely a pretext to justify the search.

Automobiles

Special rules pertaining to automobile searches have been fashioned in response to the general considerations discussed briefly in Chapter 6.* The speed and mobility of automobiles often make application for a search warrant impracticable. In an early case involving the transportation of bootleg whiskey, the Supreme Court observed:

> ...[T]he guaranty of freedom from unreasonable searches and seizures by the Fourth Amendment has been construed, practically since the beginning of the Government, as recognizing a necessary difference between a search of a store, dwelling house or other structure in respect of which a proper official warrant readily may be obtained, and a search of a ship, motor boat, wagon or automobile, for contraband goods, where it is not practicable to secure a warrant because the vehicle can be quickly moved out of the locality or jurisdiction in which the warrant must be sought.[5]

Also, automobiles are primarily a means of transporting persons or things on public highways. Although they are often used to transport things privately or for private activities, the element of privacy, the Supreme Court has said, is subsidiary and nonessential.[6] Motor vehicles are subject to extensive regulation and inspection and are observed by the police and the public generally all the time. Their public nature lessens the invasion of privacy from a search. On these bases, the Supreme Court has concluded that a search of an automobile without a warrant is reasonable and is permitted by the Fourth Amendment in two kinds of situations.

Chambers v. Maroney

"During the night of May 20... a Gulf service station in North Braddock, Pennsylvania, was robbed by two

---

*Here, as in Chapter 6, the discussion applies to automobiles as well as other vehicles with comparable characteristics.

men, each of whom carried and displayed a gun. The robbers took the currency from the cash register; the service station attendant, one Stephen Kovacich, was directed to place the coins in his right-hand glove, which was then taken by the robbers. Two teen-agers, who had earlier noticed a blue compact station wagon circling the block in the vicinity of the Gulf station, then saw the station wagon speed away from a parking lot close to the Gulf station. About the same time, they learned that the Gulf station had been robbed. They reported to police, who arrived immediately, that four men were in the station wagon and one was wearing a green sweater. Kovacich told the police that one of the men who robbed him was wearing a green sweater and the other was wearing a trench coat. A description of the car and the two robbers was broadcast over the police radio. Within an hour, a light blue compact station wagon answering the description and carrying four men was stopped by the police about two miles from the Gulf station.... [Chambers] was one of the men in the station wagon. He was wearing a green sweater and there was a trench coat in the car. The occupants were arrested and the car was driven to the police station. In the course of a thorough search of the car at the station, the police found concealed in a compartment under the dashboard two .38-caliber revolvers (one loaded with dumdum bullets), a right-hand glove containing small change, and certain cards bearing the name of Raymond Havicon, the attendant at a Boron service station in McKeesport, Pennsylvania, who had been robbed at gunpoint...."[7]

The information given to the police, including the description of the car and the robbers, unquestionably gave the arresting officers probable cause to believe that the four men in the stopped car had robbed the service station. Since the robbery had been committed only a short while before, there was also probable cause to believe that evidence of the crime, the guns used in committing it or the stolen money, was still inside the car. The Supreme Court concluded that in those circumstances, the Fourth Amendment did not prohibit the officers from making an immediate search of the car without a search warrant, to recover the evidence. Furthermore, since it was reasonable to remove the car to the police station before searching it, the officers could make the search there some time after the arrest, still without a warrant.*

The facts favoring a search in this case were unusually strong. The car was already in police custody, because the driver and occupants had been arrested. A serious crime had been committed very recently, and the car used in the crime was stopped almost during the getaway. If officers had arrested the robbers away from their car and later had located it parked on the street, and if there were no reason to believe that it would be moved or that evidence would be removed from it before a search warrant could be obtained, most of the reasons supporting a search without a warrant would not have been applicable. It is not clear whether the Fourth Amendment permits a search without a warrant in such circumstances. Probably a warrantless search is permissible if the car remains movable and the search is made promptly after officers have learned facts giving them probable cause for the search. On the other hand, if the search is postponed without any special reason for delay, then a warrant will be required to search later. Given the uncertainty of the constitutional rules, if officers have probable cause to search an automobile over which they do not already have custody, the wise course is to obtain a warrant to search, if it is practicable to do so without risking loss of the evidence.

The rule authorizing a search of an automobile without a warrant in these circumstances should be distinguished carefully from the rule authorizing a search of the passenger area of an automobile incident to the arrest of an occupant (see pp. 76–77 above). The latter rule does not depend on the existence of probable cause for the search; it is a direct consequence of the arrest. In contrast, the search of the automobile in the *Chambers* case was made after the arrest in another place, and was not incident to the arrest; it was based rather on probable cause to believe that evidence of the crime was within the automobile. Unlike a search incident to an arrest, which is limited to the area within the arrested person's control,

---

*The factors that made removal of the car to the station reasonable were that all the occupants had been arrested, a search at the time and place of the arrest would have been impractical and perhaps unsafe, and the car itself was protected by removal to a safe place.

a search based on probable cause can extend beyond the passenger area and can include the trunk and other similar places. However, while compartments of the car itself, like the glove compartment and trunk, can be opened, separate containers like luggage, a box, or even a closed paper bag cannot, unless because of their shape or because they are transparent or not fully closed or for some similar reason, they reveal contents subject to seizure. This is because a closed container, the Supreme Court has said, has an element of privacy not ordinarily attached to cars themselves, even if the container is carried in a car.[8] If such a container is found and there is probable cause to believe that it contains evidence of a crime, the officer can retain custody of it and seek a warrant to open and search it.

The contrast, then, between a search incident to the arrest of an occupant of a car and a search of a car based on probable cause can be summarized as follows:

Search incident to an arrest:

    i.   must be substantially at the time and place of arrest;

    ii.   limited to passenger area;

    iii.   can include all containers within passenger area.

Search based on probable cause:

    i.   does not need to be at the same time and place as an arrest;

    ii.   not limited to passenger area;

    iii.   does not include search of separate containers within automobile.

South Dakota v. Opperman

"Local ordinances prohibit parking in certain areas of downtown Vermillion, S.D., between the hours of 2:00 a.m. and 6:00 a.m. During the early morning hours of December 10...a Vermillion police officer observed... [Opperman's] unoccupied vehicle illegally parked in the restricted zone. At approximately 3:00 a.m., the officer issued an overtime parking ticket and placed it on the car's windshield. The citation warned: 'Vehicles in violation of any parking ordinance may be towed from the area.'

"At approximately 10 o'clock on the same morning another officer issued a second ticket for an overtime parking violation. These circumstances were routinely reported to police headquarters, and after the vehicle was inspected, the car was towed to the city impound lot.

"From outside the car at the impound lot, a police officer observed a watch on the dashboard and other items of personal property located on the back seat and back floorboard. At the officer's direction, the car door was then unlocked and, using a standard inventory form pursuant to standard police procedures, the officer inventoried the contents of the car, including the contents of the glove compartment, which was unlocked. There he found marijuana contained in a plastic bag. All items, including the contraband, were removed to the police department for safekeeping. During the late afternoon of December 10...[Opperman] appeared at the police department to claim his property. The marijuana was retained by police."[9]

In this case, unlike the *Chambers* case, there was not probable cause for a search of Opperman's car. When the officer entered the car, he was not searching for evidence of a crime; he was carrying out a standard procedure for inventorying its contents. The Supreme Court observed that such caretaking measures for impounded vehicles are routinely carried out by police throughout the country for several purposes: to protect the owner's property, to protect the police department against claims of missing property, and to protect against danger from a vehicle's contents. Officers may also look inside an impounded car to see whether it was stolen and later abandoned. The reasonableness of a search without a warrant for such purposes, the Court said, is indicated by the fact that the practice is so common. Accordingly, the Fourth Amendment does not prohibit it.

In the *Chambers* case, the reasonableness of the search depended on the fact that the officers had probable cause to search the car in which the robbers were arrested. The search could be as thorough as the particular circumstances indicated. In *Opperman*, the search was reasonable for the opposite reason; it was a routine inventory search, carried out in a routine manner. When a car has been impounded and there is *not* probable cause for a search, an examination of the car and its contents that exceeds what is ordinarily done is not justified. For example, if the usual practice when a car is towed to the police lot is only to make sure that valuable items are not visible inside, roll up windows, and lock the car, a search of the glove compartment, as in *Opperman*, would not be lawful. Even if it is routine to prepare an inventory of the contents, officers cannot make a different kind of search because of a suspicion, not amounting to probable cause, that evidence of a crime might be found. If an officer finds a closed container while making an inventory search, he should not open it and examine its contents unless the ordinary purposes of an inventory could not otherwise be accomplished and routine inventory procedure so provides. If it is practicable, the container should be left undisturbed (unless there is probable cause for a search and a warrant is obtained). The separate interest in the privacy of such a container distinguishes it from the car itself.

These principles give police authority to deal effectively with motor vehicles without disregarding those aspects of privacy protected by the Fourth Amendment. Although the authority upheld in *Chambers* and *Opperman* is extensive, neither alone nor together do those cases allow the police to search an automobile at their own discretion. Even so, many people have argued that current interpretation of the law gives officers too much authority to search automobiles. If they have probable cause, it is argued, they should nevertheless be required to obtain a search warrant unless there is an emergency that allows no time to do so; in a case like *Chambers*, having taken the car to the station, the police could and should have obtained a warrant before searching. And in cases like *Opperman*, routine security or inventory procedures may be only a pretext for an exploratory search for evidence of a crime without probable cause; it would be just as easy to secure the car and its contents without going through private property inside the glove compartment, the trunk, or elsewhere.

The continuing controversy surrounding the principles that allow a search of an automobile without a warrant emphasizes the importance of establishing clear probable cause for a search, if its primary purpose is to obtain evidence of crime. When there is doubt, it is advisable to take the added precaution of obtaining a warrant, especially if evidence that is likely to be found may be critical to a subsequent prosecution. Similarly, officers making a routine search according to a standard procedure should adhere closely to what is prescribed and not extend the procedure beyond its usual bounds.

Jailhouse Search

A search at the time and place of an arrest is likely to be limited to weapons or means of escape and obvious items of evidence that might be destroyed. Not until after the person has been brought to the station is there usually an opportunity for a careful search and examination of all the items in his possession. Sometimes, an item's significance as evidence is not plain at the time of the arrest and is revealed as the investigation proceeds. While police continue to have lawful custody of a person, a search or examination of his clothing and items on his person when he was arrested is generally permitted, even if a substantial time has passed since the arrest.

United States v. Edwards

"Shortly after 11:00 p.m....Edwards was lawfully arrested on the streets of Lebanon, Ohio, and charged with attempting to break into that city's Post Office. He was taken to the local jail and placed in a cell. Contemporaneously or shortly thereafter, investigation at the scene revealed that the attempted entry had been made through a wooden window which apparently had been pried up with a pry bar, leaving paint chips on the window sill and wire mesh screen. The next morning, trousers and a T-shirt were purchased for Edwards to substitute for the clothing which he had been wearing at the time of and since his arrest. His clothing was then taken from him and held as evidence. Examination of the clothing revealed paint chips matching the samples that had been taken from the window."[10]

The Supreme Court concluded that the removal and examination of Edwards' clothing—a search and seizure for purposes of the Fourth Amendment—was lawful. In the first place, Edwards' person and the property in his possession could have been searched at the time and place of the arrest. Such a search, the Court said, can be made also "at the station house after the arrest has occurred at another place and if evidence of crime is discovered, it may be seized and admitted in evidence."[11] Second, it is routine administrative procedure to remove personal effects that are evidence of crime before a person is placed in a cell. A reasonable delay in carrying out that procedure does not alter it or deprive the police of their authority. Furthermore, while Edwards was lawfully in custody, the police also had lawful custody of the things on his person when he was arrested; at least for a reasonable time, those things could be examined and if they were evidence of crime, they could be seized. An arrest, as the more significant interference with a person's liberty, has the effect of temporarily interrupting the privacy ordinarily protected by the Fourth Amendment, so far as items in his possession at the time of the arrest are concerned.

While an arrested person is in police custody, therefore, officers have extensive authority to search his possessions at the time of the arrest. In general, if officers have reason to examine such items, whether because of particular facts in that case or because of a routine procedure, and if the examination is carried out without unnecessary imposition, it is allowed. Such a search may not be employed to harrass the person or simply to display the authority of the police. The occasional practice of handling or mishandling a person's possessions in order to impress on him the value of cooperating with the police is highly improper. And once a person has been surrendered to a magistrate or released, the authority to search based on custody ends.

Hot Pursuit and Other Exigent Circumstances

Warden v. Hayden

"About 8:00 a.m....an armed robber entered the business premises of the Diamond Cab Company in Baltimore, Maryland. He took some $363 and ran. Two cab drivers in the vicinity, attracted by shouts of 'Holdup,' followed the man to 2111 Cocoa Lane. One driver notified the company dispatcher by radio that the man was a Negro about 5'8" tall, wearing a light cap and dark jacket, and that he had entered the house on Cocoa Lane. The dispatcher relayed the information to police who were proceeding to the scene of the robbery. Within minutes, police arrived at the house in a number of patrol cars. An officer knocked and announced their presence. Mrs. Hayden answered, and the officers told her they believed that a robber had entered the house, and asked to search the house. She offered no objection.

"The officers spread out through the first and second floors and the cellar in search of the robber. Hayden was found in an upstairs bedroom feigning sleep. He was arrested when the officers on the first floor and in the cellar reported that no other man was in the house. Meanwhile an officer was attracted to an adjoining bathroom by the noise of running water, and discovered a shotgun and a pistol in a flush tank; another officer... found in a washing machine a jacket and trousers of the type the fleeing man was said to have worn. A clip of ammunition for the pistol and a cap were found under the mattress of Hayden's bed, and ammunition for the shotgun was found in a bureau drawer in Hayden's room."[12]

Police are not ordinarily allowed to enter private premises without a warrant unless the owner or occupant consents.* Here, however, the officers who entered the house at 2111 Cocoa Lane were in pursuit of someone who had committed an armed robbery a few minutes before. Their entry was as much a performance of their peace-keeping function as it was investigative. In those circumstances, the entry and search of the house were lawful. "The Fourth Amendment does not require police

*Mrs. Hayden's failure to object to the entry should not be regarded as consent to the search (see Chapter 9).

officers to delay in the course of an investigation if to do so would gravely endanger their lives or the lives of others. Speed here was essential, and only a thorough search of the house for persons and weapons could have ensured that Hayden was the only man present and that the police had control of all weapons which could be used against them or to effect an escape.''[13]

The conclusion that the officers were authorized to enter the house in pursuit of Hayden is an application of a general principle that we considered earlier. When the police are performing their peace-keeping function, an interference with private persons is reasonable, provided that the interference is necessary to the performance of that function and goes no further than the necessity (and provided also that the function is one that ought to be performed in the circumstances). Just as an officer can enter a building in response to a cry for help or the unexplained sound of a gunshot without postponing action until he has obtained a search warrant, he is not required to abandon the pursuit of someone who he reasonably believes has just committed a serious crime if the person enters a private house. It would give most people little security to think that police could not carry out their responsibility in such circumstances.

This exception to the requirement of a search warrant is sometimes called the ''hot pursuit'' exception, because of the *Hayden* case. The rule applies generally, however, to any emergency situation in which the police must act before a warrant can be obtained, whether the emergency involves danger to persons within or, as in *Hayden*, the pursuit of a criminal. More troublesome is the question whether officers can enter private premises without a warrant solely to prevent the destruction of evidence of crime. If the police are not responsible for the creation of the emergency, either by provoking the destruction of the evidence or by failing to obtain a search warrant while there was time to do so, a warrantless entry is allowed. Particularly in this case, however, an officer entering premises without a warrant should have strong grounds for belief that immediate action is needed. A warrantless entry is not authorized simply because there is probable cause to believe that evidence of crime is on the premises and might be destroyed before a warrant is obtained.

Although a professional police officer does not hesitate to act in a clear emergency, it is not always easy in a stressful situation to decide whether the circumstances authorize an entry of private premises. The conditions that must be met for an entry without a warrant are the following:

1. *There must be a solid basis for the belief that an emergency exists.*

2. *The emergency must be serious and substantial.*

3. *The emergency must not allow delay long enough to obtain a warrant.*

4. *The officer making the search or other officers must not be responsible for the existence of the emergency.*

5. *The search must not exceed the need created by the emergency, including necessary precautionary measures for the safety of the officer(s) and others.*

Seizure

The Fourth Amendment is principally concerned with the protection of privacy against unreasonable searches and not with what can be seized during a lawful search. Of course, an officer conducting a lawful search cannot seize anything at all. Among the categories of things that have always been subject to seizure are contraband, which is not lawfully in private possession, and the fruits and instruments of crime. Evidence of a crime also can be seized, even if it is not contraband or a fruit or instrument of the crime. Often, an officer will discover something that he suspects is evidence of a crime. Certainty is not required. He must, however, have a reasonable basis for his suspicion. Here as elsewhere in Fourth Amendment law, the standard of probable cause applies.

In some of the situations that we considered in this chapter, the officer conducting a search was looking for particular evidence. In *Chambers*, for example, officers searching the car expected to find evidence of the robbery at the service station. And in *Edwards*, the officers expected to find on Edwards's clothing paint from the window where the break-in occurred. In many cases of search without a warrant, the officer conducting the search does not have a particular expectation. As we saw, a search incident to an arrest or a search of the possessions of a person who is detained in police custody is lawful without special reason to believe that anything will be found. Similarly, in *Opperman*, there was no reason to suppose before the search that marijuana would be found.

Whether or not officers are searching for something in particular, they may unexpectedly discover evidence of a crime. The officers in *Chambers* might have found narcotics in the car along with the weapons. (In fact, they did find evidence of another service station robbery, for which they were not looking. See page 79 above.) The basic rule in such situations is that if the search is lawful, it makes no difference that the item is not what the officer expected to find or that the person whom it incriminates is not the person he suspected.* An officer lawfully engaged in the performance of his duties can seize evidence of a crime; so long as the search or other activity in which he is engaged when he finds the evidence violates no right under the Fourth Amendment, the seizure itself raises no Fourth Amendment issues.

In Chapter 2, we considered the rule that only a defendant whose own constitutional rights have been violated can challenge the admission of evidence in a criminal case. So, to take an extreme example, if the police unlawfully broke into the home of one person and found evidence incriminating another, who had no connection with the searched premises, the evidence could be used at trial against the latter. His constitutional rights were not invaded by the unlawful search.** (No doubt the courts would react differently if a police department were deliberately to set out on a pattern of such conduct and repeatedly violate the Fourth Amendment). While this rule may occasionally benefit the prosecution, it does not affect the guiding principles for the police, whose professional responsibility requires them to follow

---

*For the application of this rule to searches on a warrant, which is required to state the particular items to be seized, see pp. 104–105 below.

**If the evidence were found in a trunk belonging to the defendant which he had left in the other person's house for safekeeping, the search of the trunk would invade the defendant's privacy and he would be able to challenge admission of the evidence against him.

the Constitution. They do not meet that responsibility if they act otherwise, even if evidence is ultimately not excluded.

Summary

The rules discussed in this chapter give the police extensive authority to search persons and places whenever a search is necessary to the performance of their regular duties. In situations when they have probable cause but do not have an opportunity to obtain a warrant before searching, or when a search is a standard procedure accompanying the performance of another function, a warrant authorizing the search is not required. That is not a general authorization to search whenever a search might be useful. In each case, the rule allowing a search without a warrant contains its own limits, with respect both to the situations in which it applies and to the extent of the search that is allowed. Officers can avoid challenges to a search and keep their actions within constitutional bounds if they remember that every such search is an invasion of the privacy protected by the Fourth Amendment and that it should extend no further than appears reasonably necessary for the performance of substantial and specific duties.

Questions for Discussion

1. What does the phrase "search and seizure" mean under the Fourth Amendment?

2. If an officer watches a person's movements on the street and picks up something that the person has dropped, why is that not a search and seizure under the Fourth Amendment?

3. What is a search "incident to an arrest"?
   In what circumstances is a search incident to an arrest allowed?
   Why is a search incident to an arrest allowed without a warrant?
   What is the difference between a search incident to an arrest and a frisk?

How do the circumstances in which each is allowed differ?

How extensive is a search incident to an arrest?

How extensive is a search incident to an arrest of an occupant of an automobile?

4. In what circumstances can an officer who stops a driver for a moving traffic violation search the person?

5. What are the reasons for treating a search of a private motor vehicle differently from a search of private premises?

6. What two general principles authorize the search of a motor vehicle without a warrant?
   Explain the difference between them.

7. Is probable cause needed for an inventory search of a car that is impounded by the police and removed to a police lot?

8. After a person has been booked and placed in a detention cell, is a further search of his person or items in his possession at the time of the arrest allowed?
   What limits are there on such a search?

9. In what kinds of emergencies are officers allowed to enter and search private premises without a warrant?
   What limits are there on such a search?
   Give examples of the limits that are relevant to different kinds of emergencies.

10. What things discovered during a lawful search can be seized?

Problem Cases

1. Police officers arrested Smith pursuant to an arrest warrant charging him with the theft of automobile tires. At the time of their arrest, an officer removed Smith's wallet from his pocket. After Smith had been taken to the police station, his wallet was searched thoroughly. Stolen checks, unrelated to the stolen tires, were found in the wallet and seized.

Were the checks lawfully seized? If so, on what theory?

2. Three officers having a warrant to arrest Jones for narcotics offenses entered his apartment and found him lying on a couch watching television. There was a small table at the end of the couch near his head. As they made the arrest, one of the officers picked up a cigar box on the table and opened it. Jones's wallet was inside the box. The officer looked inside the wallet and found papers incriminating Jones, which he seized.[14]

Were the papers lawfully seized?

3. While investigating the theft of a car, officers located the transmission of the stripped car inside a garage. They were able to see the transmission from the street by looking through a window of the garage. Later that same day, they arrested three men as the men were leaving the garage.[15]

Could the officers then enter the garage without a search warrant and remove the transmission and other evidence inside?

4. An officer stopped Green, who was driving his car above the speed limit. While the officer was writing a ticket, he saw Green remove a small package from the glove compartment and place it in a pocket of his jacket. Suspecting that the package contained narcotics, the officer went to the window of Green's car and directed him to get out. He then frisked Green, removed the package, and opened it. Finding an envelope that appeared to contain narcotics, he arrested Green for possession of narcotics and took him to the station.

Was the arrest lawful?

5. Officers stopped Young, who was driving his car above the speed limit. He was unable to produce a driver's license. The officers arrested him and placed him in the rear of their car. One officer then opened a rear door of Young's car and looked inside. On the floor, he saw a sealed manila envelope. He opened the envelope and found inside a number of credit cards made out in different names. Having reason to believe that the cards were stolen and suspecting that additional stolen goods might be found in the trunk, the officer opened it. Searching inside, he found stolen goods.

Were the search of the rear of Young's car, the manila envelope, and the trunk of his car lawful?

6. Officers arrested Brown for driving while intoxicated. At a nearby service station, Brown called his brother, who came to the station. Brown asked his brother to drive the car home. The police refused to let the car be driven away and impounded it. The next day, an officer made an inventory search of the car and found drugs.[16]

Was the search lawful?

7. Reuben was arrested for the murder of a child. There was reason to believe that he had taken the child in his car and killed him. On the day after the arrest, an officer saw Reuben's car legally parked on the street. He looked through the window and saw what appeared to be blood stains on the rear seat. The officer had the car towed to the police station, where it was thoroughly searched. Evidence against Reuben, including the blood stains, was found.[17]

Was the search of the car lawful?

8. Postal authorities suspected Miller of having stolen items from the mail. He was advised of the pending investigation but was not arrested. Learning that Miller was on his way to his locker in the post office building, an investigator opened the locker with a master key and searched inside. He found a number of stolen items.

Was the search of the locker lawful?

9. On the day after a robbery was committed at a grocery store, the police were given reliable information that the robber was staying at a particular house. Officers went to the house and asked a woman who came to the door if they could enter to look for the robbery suspect. She refused to give permission. The officers informed her that they would search anyway and entered over her protest. They found the suspect in an upstairs room and arrested him.

Were the entry and search lawful?

10. Jackson was arrested on a robbery charge. While he was in custody, officers broke into his house and made a thorough search. In various places around the house, they found the fruits of several unsolved robberies. An officer searching in an upstairs closet found clothing that he recognized as similar to the description of clothing worn by the victim of a recent kidnapping. The robbery fruits and the clothing were seized and taken to police headquarters.

Was the seizure of the fruits of the robbery lawful?
Was the seizure of the clothing lawful?

Jackson was prosecuted for robbery.

Can the items seized at his house be used in evidence against him?

An examination of the kidnapping victim's clothing, which had been left in Jackson's house by someone else, produced evidence that incriminated Shaw. Shaw did not live in Jackson's house and had not been inside it in several months. He was prosecuted for the kidnapping.

Can the clothing be used against Shaw at the trial?

Notes

1. Chimel v. California, 395 U.S. 752, 762–63 (1969).
2. United States v. Chadwick, 433 U.S. 1, 15 (1977).
3. United States v. Chadwick, *supra* note 2.
4. New York v. Belton, ___ U.S. ___ (1981).
5. Carroll v. United States, 267 U.S. 132, 153 (1925).
6. See South Dakota v. Opperman, 428 U.S. 364 (1976); Cady v. Dombrowski, 413 U.S. 433 (1973); *cf.* United States v. Chadwick, 433 U.S. 1, 12–13 (1977).
7. Chambers v. Maroney, 399 U.S. 42, 44 (1970).
8. Arkansas v. Sanders, 442 U.S. 753 (1979); Robbins v. California, ___ U.S. ___ (1981).
9. South Dakota v. Opperman, 428 U.S. 364, 365–66 (1976) (footnote omitted).

10. United States v. Edwards, 415 U.S. 800, 801–802 (1974) (footnote omitted).

11. *Id.* at 803 (footnote omitted).

12. Warden v. Hayden, 387 U.S. 294, 297–98 (1967) (footnote omitted).

13. *Id.* at 298–99.

14. See United States v. Harrison, 461 F.2d 1127 (5th Cir. 1972).

15. See United States v. Wright, 449 F.2d 1355 (D.C. Cir. 1971).

16. See State v. Goodrich, 256 N.W.2d 506 (Minn. 1977).

17. See Smith v. Slayton, 484 F.2d 1188 (4th Cir. 1973).

CHAPTER 8

SEARCH AND SEIZURE: WITH A SEARCH WARRANT

In the last chapter, we discussed exceptions to the principle requiring that a search be made pursuant to a search warrant. The exceptions arise when a search is a reasonable and routine or necessary part of the performance of another official duty; it is the arrest, or impounding of a vehicle, or pursuit of a criminal that dispenses with the requirement of a warrant. In this chapter, we shall consider the constitutional law applicable to a search when the discovery and seizure of evidence, including contraband or the fruits of a crime, are the main objective.*

The Requirement of a Warrant

In the absence of some other justification for a search that makes it reasonable, the second clause of the Fourth Amendment applies:

> ...[N]o warrants, shall issue, but upon probable cause, supported by oath or affirmation, and particularly describing the place to be searched, and the persons or things to be seized.

*Although a search without a warrant may be permitted to prevent the destruction of evidence, see p. 88 above, the critical factor is the emergency created by the danger that evidence will be destroyed rather than simply the purpose to obtain evidence.

Not only does this provision indicate that a warrant is required; it also indicates with considerable precision how a valid warrant is issued and what it contains.

A search warrant is a formal authorization by a judicial officer to conduct a specific search. Within constitutional limits federal, state, and local law provide who may issue a warrant. Usually, any judge within the jurisdiction is competent to do so. The Constitution requires that the person issuing a warrant "be neutral and detached, and...capable of determining whether probable cause exists for the requested arrest or search."[1] The requirement of neutrality is illustrated by a case in which the Supreme Court held that a search warrant could not be issued by the Attorney General of a state, who was directing the investigation of a murder and expected to be the chief prosecutor at trial.[2] Although he had legal training, he did not have the necessary neutrality because of his involvement in the investigation and prosecution. On the other hand, where local law so provided, the clerk of a municipal court was allowed to issue an arrest warrant in a traffic case; although he was not a lawyer, he was a neutral official and was capable of making the determination of probable cause.[3]

It is reasonable to ask why a judicial official who is not a specialist in criminal investigation should decide whether a search is proper, rather than a professional investigative official. The reason is the point made in Chapter 1: the Fourth Amendment declares that the value of individual automony and privacy competes with the social value of investigating crime, and that the two values have to be balanced. Because a police officer is professionally engaged in criminal investigation, he is likely sometimes to overemphasize that side of the balance, the more so if he believes that the person whose privacy is at stake has committed a crime. Accordingly, when there is not an emergency requiring immediate action, it is preferable for the balance to be made by someone whose perspective is neutral and whose profession regularly requires him to weigh conflicting interests.

If there is clearly probable cause for a search, it may seem like a needless and time-consuming formality to insist that a warrant be obtained. Whatever the officer's view of the facts, the warrant gives assurance that constitutional requirements are met. A cautious officer

Figure 8-1a.
Search Warrant (Front)
[Opposite]

United States District Court

FOR THE

UNITED STATES OF AMERICA

vs.

Docket No.

Case No.

SEARCH WARRANT

To

Affidavit(s) having been made before me by

that he has reason to believe that { on the person of / on the premises known as }

in the   District of

there is now being concealed certain property, namely

here describe property

and as I am satisfied that there is probable cause to believe that the property so described is being concealed on the person or premises above described and that grounds for application for issuance of the search warrant exist as stated in the supporting affidavit(s).

You are hereby commanded to search within a period of _____ (not to exceed 10 days) the person or place named for the property specified, serving this warrant and making the search { in the daytime (6:00 a.m. to 10:00 p.m.) / at any time in the day or night* } and if the property be found there to seize it, leaving a copy of this warrant and receipt for the property taken, and prepare a written inventory of the property seized and promptly return this warrant and bring the property before _____ as required by law.

     Federal judge or magistrate

Dated this   day of   , 19

_____,
Judge (Federal or State Court of Record) or Federal Magistrate.

*The Federal Rules of Criminal Procedure provide: "The warrant shall be served in the daytime, unless the issuing authority, by appropriate provision in the warrant, and for reasonable cause shown, authorizes its execution at times other than daytime." (Rule 41(c)). A statement of grounds for reasonable cause should be made in the affidavit(s) if a search is to be authorized "at any time day or night" pursuant to Rule 41(c).

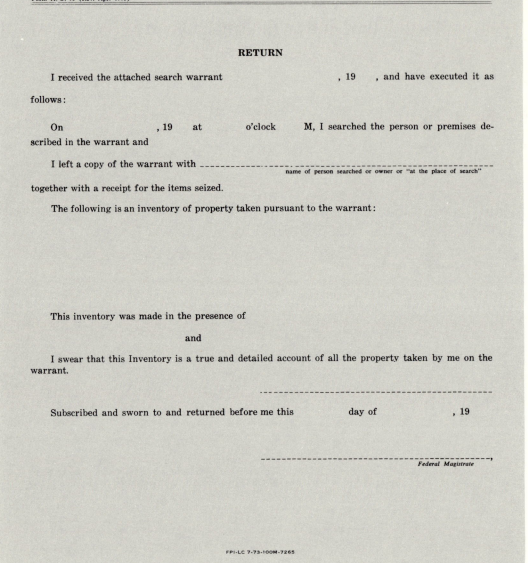

RETURN

I received the attached search warrant   , 19   , and have executed it as follows:

On   , 19   at   o'clock   M, I searched the person or premises described in the warrant and

I left a copy of the warrant with _____
                                                                    name of person searched or owner or "at the place of search"

together with a receipt for the items seized.

The following is an inventory of property taken pursuant to the warrant:

This inventory was made in the presence of

                                   and

I swear that this Inventory is a true and detailed account of all the property taken by me on the warrant.

Subscribed and sworn to and returned before me this   day of   , 19

                        --,
                                                                    Federal Magistrate

FPI-LC 7-73-100M-7265

Figure 8-1b.
Search Warrant (Back)

who is at all uncertain whether a search without a warrant is authorized, will obtain a warrant if there is time and opportunity. In the *Chadwick* case (p. 75), for example, even though the federal agents believed that they were allowed to search the trunk without a warrant, nothing would have been lost had they taken that further precaution; had they obtained a warrant, critical evidence for the prosecution would not have been suppressed.

100

The issuance of a warrant confirms the officer's judgment that a search is proper. In close cases, when the existence of probable cause is not altogether clear, a court may be more inclined to uphold a search if a warrant was obtained, because the officer's good faith is evident. More generally, if it is the regular practice of a police department to obtain search warrants, the courts of that jurisdiction will have more reason to accept the necessity of acting without a warrant in some cases.

Probable Cause

The meaning of probable cause was examined in connection with arrest in Chapter 3. Its meaning is the same when a search is in question: the officer applying for a warrant must have information that would lead a reasonable person to conclude that something subject to seizure is at the premises to be searched. Any kind of information, including personal observations, hearsay reports, or a reliable informer's tips, can be used, provided that altogether it provides a basis for the magistrate's independent judgment. The Constitution requires that this information be given under "oath or affirmation." Ordinarily, it is given in a sworn, written affidavit. Federal law and many state laws provide for the issuance of a search warrant by telephone if it is impracticable to appear in person before the magistrate; the information is given orally under oath and recorded, and a written affidavit containing the information is prepared later.

The Place To Be Searched

The Fourth Amendment provides expressly that a warrant shall describe "particularly" the place to be searched. That provision prevents issuance of a warrant so broad that searchers could rummage at will through a number of private places, effectively defeating the purpose of requiring them to obtain a warrant. The requirement of particularity clearly is not satisfied by a warrant to search all the houses on a block or a warrant specifying

United States District Court

FOR THE

_____

UNITED STATES OF AMERICA

vs.

Docket No._____

Case No._____

AFFIDAVIT FOR
SEARCH WARRANT

BEFORE

Name of Judge¹ or Federal Magistrate   Address of Judge¹ or Federal Magistrate

The undersigned being duly sworn deposes and says:

That he has reason to believe that (on the person of)
(on the premises known as)

in the   District of

there is now being concealed certain property, namely

here describe property

which are

here give alleged grounds for search and seizure²

And that the facts tending to establish the foregoing grounds for issuance of a Search Warrant are as follows:³

---,
Signature of Affiant.

---,
Official Title, if any.

Sworn to before me, and subscribed in my presence,   , 19

---,
Judge¹ or Federal Magistrate.

¹United States Judge or Judge of a State Court of Record.
²If a search is to be authorized "at any time in the day or night" pursuant to Rule 41(c), show reasonable cause therefor.
³If the warrant is to authorize execution pursuant to 21 U.S.C. § 879 without prior notice of authority or purpose, indicate the circumstances creating the need for such a warrant.

FPI-LOM-11-78-50M 1799

102

Figure 8-2.
Affidavit for Search Warrant

only the street address of an apartment building containing fifty apartments. On the other hand, an officer applying for a search warrant is not expected to know exactly where in a house a particular item is concealed; it is anticipated that he will have to search to find the things to be seized.

Ordinarily, the place to be searched is adequately described if it is limited to a single dwelling unit: a one-family house, or one-family unit in a two- or three-family house, or a single apartment in a building. A single dwelling unit may include several structures, like a house, garage, and tool shed. Although the easiest and most common description is the address of the premises, including if necessary the apartment number or floor of a house, any description that unambiguously identifies the place to be searched is sufficient.

Difficult questions may arise when premises are not clearly divided into distinct dwelling units. Suppose that an elderly couple share a house with their married daughter. Each couple occupies separate rooms, but some rooms are used in common. The single address, the family relationship, and the common use of some rooms support issuance of a warrant to search the entire premises. The separate use of other rooms, however, suggests an arrangement more like two apartments. Separate entrances would also indicate that there were really two apartments. In such a case, the warrant should identify the premises to be searched as precisely as circumstances permit. If it is arguable that the warrant covers more than one dwelling unit, the officer seeking the warrant should be prepared to show that the premises are commonly treated as one and that a more limited identification is impracticable. So long as the more inclusive description is fairly explained by the unified nature of the premises rather than a failure to ascertain which of two or more distinct premises is appropriately searched, the warrant is valid.

The Things To Be Seized

The Fourth Amendment provides also that a search warrant shall describe "particularly" the things to be seized. The point of this provision is to prevent officials from making a general search through all the contents of private premises, with the unspecific hope of finding something. A search pursuant to a warrant is permitted only if searchers have probable cause to believe that particular items subject to seizure will be found.

The requirement of particularity is interpreted according to the nature of the items and the circumstances. If police are investigating a specific crime, it may be practicable to specify a weapon or particular items of clothing as the object of a search. If they are looking for the fruits of one or several burglaries, it may be practicable only to provide a list of missing items. On the other hand, a warrant that referred to "stolen goods" without any specification at all would not be valid. If a search is to be made of premises where a gambling or narcotics operation is conducted, a general description such as "gambling devices" or "narcotics and narcotics paraphernalia" is usually enough. If the items in question might easily be confused with similar items not subject to seizure, the requirement of particularity is applied more strictly. A warrant to search for evidence of fraudulent business transactions, for example, would not be adequate if it specified simply "business records."

In Chapter 7, we noted some situations in which an officer conducting a lawful search unexpectedly found something subject to seizure. The general rule, we saw, is that if a search is lawful, any item discovered during the search that is subject to seizure can be seized. The same rule applies to searches on a warrant, even though the warrant describes specific items as the object of the search. For example, while executing a warrant to search for narcotics, an officer discovers credit cards assigned in different names; he recognizes one of the names as that of a person who was recently robbed. Since the search is lawful and there is probable cause to believe that the credit cards are evidence of crime, the officer can seize them even though they were not named in the warrant.

It is important to distinguish between items that are the *object* of a search on a warrant and items that are found incidentally or unexpectedly. Because the Fourth Amendment provides expressly that the things to be seized must be listed particularly, all the items that are the object of a search must be listed in the warrant. In the case above, if the officer were searching for both narcotics and stolen credit cards but had failed to list the latter in

the warrant, the requirement of particularity would not be met and the search for the credit cards would not be valid.*

*In such a case, it may be impossible to say that the search was for one and not the other of the items sought. If the officer had found the narcotics listed in the warrant and then continued to search for the credit cards, the object of the latter search would be clear and, unless the credit cards were included in the warrant, the search would be unlawful.

Scope of the Search

The permissible scope of a search on a warrant is determined by the descriptions of the place to be searched and the things to be seized. Searchers may look anywhere in the specified place where the things sought might be found. If they are stolen checks, it would be proper to look in a desk, a dresser, or a shoebox in a closet, since checks might be concealed in any of those places. But if only stolen tires were listed in the warrant, none of those places could be searched, since none of them could possibly hold tires. Similarly, once the things specified in a warrant have been found, the search authorized by it has accomplished its objective and no further search is permitted.

So long as officers respect the limitations imposed by a valid warrant, their search will be upheld. They are not required to search the most likely hiding place first or to make subtle judgments about whether one place or another might be a hiding place. Rather, they are expected to conduct their search in good faith with the reasonableness of an ordinary person looking for specific objects within a limited area.

Persons on the Premises

Often one or more persons will be at the premises when police enter to execute a search warrant.

Ybarra v. Illinois

Officers had a warrant to search a tavern for evidence of narcotics offenses. When they arrived at the tavern, about a dozen customers were present. The officers had no information about any of them. One officer frisked the customers, while other officers searched the tavern. Heroin was found in a customer's pocket.[4]

The Supreme Court held that the frisk of the customer and seizure of the heroin were not lawful. A warrant to search a place does not ordinarily authorize a search of any person who happens to be present.* If the officer had reason to believe that the customer had concealed on his person something that would otherwise have been discovered during the search of the premises, it would have been permissible to search him. Or, as in the *Terry* case, if the officers had specific and concrete grounds for believing that a frisk was necessary to protect themselves while the search was carried out, the frisk would have been lawful. Except in circumstances like those, when there is special justification for a search of the person, a search warrant extends only to the *place* described in the warrant.

Officers who are executing a valid warrant to search for contraband** are permitted to detain occupants of the premises while the search is conducted. The warrant provides a clear basis for suspicion of criminal activity, like the basis for a frisk in *Terry*. And the limited intrusion on the liberty of the occupants is justified by the substantial law enforcement interests that are served, among which are "preventing flight in the event that incriminating evidence is found," "minimizing the risk of harm to the officers," and facilitating "the orderly completion of the search."[5]

The Conduct of a Search

The Fourth Amendment limits the occasions when a search is permitted and the scope of a search. It does not address the manner in which a search is conducted. It is not a violation of the Amendment, for example, for an officer to deal more roughly than necessary with the goods of someone whose premises are searched.

---

*In appropriate circumstances, a warrant might explicitly authorize a search of premises and named or unnamed persons present on the premises.

**It is not clear whether the same rule applies if the warrant is to search for evidence of a crime that is not contraband. If the warrant furnishes a basis for suspecting criminal activity at the premises and detention of the occupants would further substantial law enforcement interests, it would presumably be permissible.

Nonetheless, officers conducting a search should exercise their authority with as much respect for the privacy and dignity of the individual as circumstances permit. The correct performance of a public function accomplishes its objective without intruding unnecessarily on private interests. Accordingly, officers having a warrant to search ought to execute the warrant with as little disturbance as possible of persons who will be affected. Ordinarily, that will dictate a preference for a search during daytime and if practicable, when someone occupying the premises is at home. A nighttime search or a search carried out while none of the occupants is present is likely to arouse fear and resentment to a much greater degree.

A further reason for conducting a search while someone is present is that it eliminates the need for a forcible entry and reduces the likelihood of damage to the premises or their contents. Authority to search is not authority to damage or destroy needlessly. Officers conducting a search should regard it as part of their professional responsibility not to damage private property. In an extreme case, the deliberate, needless destruction of property during a search or any deliberate abuse of the authority to search would be a violation of the general constitutional right not to suffer deprivation by the government without due process of law.

Federal law and the laws of many states require that officers give notice of their authority and purpose and allow the occupant an opportunity to admit them peaceably before they make a forcible entry, which includes not only breaking in but entering without permission through a closed but unlocked door. Some judicial opinions suggest that even in the absence of a statute, the Constitution requires that notice be given before a forcible entry. There is a recognized exception to this requirement if giving notice would endanger the officers or others or invite the destruction of evidence. But, as in other situations when an emergency justifies a departure from normal practice, officers must have specific grounds to justify their actions. Aside from the requirements of the Constitution and local law, a needless forcible entry not only escalates the intrusion; also, it creates a danger to the occupants and officers alike that might be avoided.

A search pursuant to a warrant is a planned intrusion on the ordinary privacy of people and usually does not call for the swift and sudden judgments that confront police in other work. There is particular reason, therefore, for such a search to be carried out with full regard for the rights and interests of the persons involved. Even those aspects of a search that do not directly implicate the Fourth Amendment may have an effect on the outcome if the search is challenged on constitutional grounds. Deciding a close question of probable cause, a court is more likely to uphold an officer's judgment if it is evident that he was generally mindful of the rights of the individual. A search carried out with unnecessary force and destructiveness may the more easily be perceived as lacking a constitutional justification. Here, as elsewhere, the objectives of professional police work and the constitutional rights of individuals are not at odds.

Questions for Discussion

1. On what is the requirement of a search warrant based?

2. What is the general distinction between searches for which a warrant is not required and searches for which a warrant is required?

3. Who is authorized to issue a search warrant?

4. Why is a police officer or a superior officer within the police department not authorized to issue a search warrant?

5. How does probable cause for a search compare with probable cause for an arrest?

6. How should the premises to be searched be described in a warrant?

7. How should the things that are the object of a search be described in a warrant?

8. In what circumstances can an officer conducting a search on a warrant search the pockets of a person on the premises?

9. Describe the manner of a well-conducted search on a warrant.

Problem Case

Detectives working in the Fraud Division acquired evidence sufficient to establish probable cause that Swift was operating a stock swindle. A magistrate issued a search warrant authorizing them to search "any premises at which John E. Swift conducts stock market transactions" and to seize "records of stock transactions, bank statements, and other evidence of crime." Executing the warrant, officers searched a four-room office on the fifth floor of an office building at 1010 Rand Place, another two-room office in a building at 1020 Rand Place, and Swift's home, at 123 Palm Drive, in which he had a small office. Swift conducted business from all three locations. The officers seized extensive records of stock transactions from both offices. They seized statements of bank accounts in the name of Swift and others in the name of Mrs. Swift from the office at 123 Palm Drive. Searching elsewhere in the house, they found a paper bag containing marijuana in Swift's dresser in the master bedroom, and seized that.

Were the searches and seizures lawful?
Explain your answers, with respect to each search and the items seized.

Notes

1. Shadwick v. City of Tampa, 407 U.S. 345, 350 (1972).
2. Coolidge v. New Hampshire, 403 U.S. 443 (1971).
3. Shadwick v. City of Tampa, 407 U.S. 345 (1972).
4. Ybarra v. Illinois, 444 U.S. 85 (1979).
5. Michigan v. Summers, ___ U.S. ___, ___ (1981).

CHAPTER 9

SEARCH AND SEIZURE: WITH CONSENT

The Fourth Amendment does not prohibit public officials from entering private premises when the occupants are willing for them to do so. In this chapter, we shall consider circumstances in which officers can lawfully conduct a search for evidence without a warrant or any of the special justifications discussed in Chapter 7, because they have been given consent. Consent to a search is permission given by the person (or a person) whose rights under the Fourth Amendment the search would otherwise have violated.

For consent to be effective, it has to meet three tests: (1) it must be *real*; (2) it must be *given by an appropriate person*; and (3) it must be *applicable to the search in question*. All of those tests are easy to understand and apply in obvious cases:

1. We do not ordinarily say that permission to do something counts if it was obtained by threatening or physically abusing the person who gave it. Suppose that an officer rang the doorbell of a private home, knocked down the person who came to the door, and sat on his stomach while he asked for permission to search the house. Even if the person managed to gasp out the words, "Yes, It's O.K. to search," he has not really consented to the search.

2. We do not ordinarily say that permission to do something counts if it was obtained from a person who has no stake in what is to be done. Suppose that an officer wanted to search a house when no one was at home and asked a neighbor up the street if he gave his permission. Even if the neighbor replied, "Sure, go ahead," the officer has not been given

consent to search. The neighbor's consent may have been genuine enough, but it was beside the point; the premises searched were not his.

3. We do not ordinarily say that permission to do a particular thing is permission to do anything at all. If you give your neighbor permission to borrow your lawnmower, you do not expect him to drive off with your car. Similarly, an officer may be told that he can search the rooms on the first floor but not the rooms on the second floor. The consent that he has been given does not authorize him to search a bedroom on the second floor.

Officers encounter situations much more complicated than these simple examples. But it will be helpful to remember them. Even when the facts become much more complex, the questions to ask remain the same: Was consent real? Who gave it? How far does it go?

Real Consent

As we have seen, the capacity for forceful and decisive action is one of the distinguishing characteristics of police. In many situations, especially if he has already made a show of force, an officer's request for permission to search may sound like a demand or a threat to use force if permission is refused. If evidence is found that incriminates the person who gave permission, he is likely to say—and to believe—that he would not have given permission if he had thought he had any real choice and that he did not truly consent to the search. Even if an officer has acted entirely in good faith, he may have difficulty showing that he did not directly or indirectly intimidate the person on whose consent the validity of a search depends. The fact that a person used words that indicated consent may not be sufficient if he claims convincingly that he spoke only out of fear.

Schneckloth v. Bustamonte

"While on routine patrol in Sunnyvale, California, at approximately 2:40 in the morning, Police Officer James

Rand stopped an automobile when he observed that one headlight and its license plate light were burned out. Six men were in the vehicle. Joe Alcala and...Robert Bustamonte, were in the front seat with Joe Gonzales, the driver. Three older men were seated in the rear. When, in response to the policeman's question, Gonzales could not produce a driver's license, Officer Rand asked if any of the other five had any evidence of identification. Only Alcala produced a license, and he explained that the car was his brother's. After the six occupants had stepped out of the car at the officer's request and after two additional policemen had arrived, Officer Rand asked Alcala if he could search the car. Alcala replied, 'Sure, go ahead.' Prior to the search no one was threatened with arrest and, according to Officer Rand's uncontradicted testimony, it 'was all very congenial at this time.' Gonzales testified that Alcala actually helped in the search of the car, by opening the trunk and glove compartment. In Gonzales' words: '[T]he police officer asked Joe [Alcala], he goes, "Does the trunk open?" And Joe said, "Yes." He went to the car and got the keys and opened up the trunk.' Wadded up under the left rear seat, the police officers found three checks that had previously been stolen from a car wash."[1]

Bustamonte was later prosecuted, and the checks found in the car were used in evidence against him. The search of the car was justified on the ground that Alcala, who was responsible for the car at that time, had given his consent. It might easily be concluded that Alcala agreed to the search unwillingly, because the situation was threatening: it was late at night, Officer Rand had been joined by two more officers; the driver of the car carried no license; the owner of the car was not present; the car's lights were defective. On the other hand, there was no evidence to contradict Rand's testimony that the officers did not threaten or abuse any of the occupants; and Alcala's actual words and conduct indicated that he was willing to let the officers search the car. The trial court concluded that Alcala's consent was real, and the Supreme Court upheld its judgment. It is easy to see how a small difference in the facts might have led to a different result.

An officer may not be able to avoid asking for consent to search in circumstances that will raise doubts later about its genuineness. Officer Rand found himself in such a situation. No matter what he said or did, any occupant of the car against whom evidence was found probably would claim later that consent to the search was not voluntarily given. An officer should be alert to the problem and take steps to alleviate a threatening atmosphere. So far as he can he should view the situation from the other person's perspective. The more thoroughly and clearly he explains the person's rights, the more easily he will be able to show later that the person gave his consent freely and not because he believed (mistakenly) that he dare not refuse.

If an officer knows that he does not intend to use force, he may easily suppose that the person with whom he is dealing knows this also. Even so, he should avoid any action that might be interpreted as a threat to use force if permission to search is not given. In a doubtful case, it is a wise precaution to tell the person explicitly that he need not give permission to search and that nothing will happen to him if he does not. While such advice is not always required, it will count strongly in favor of upholding the search.

Of course, if an officer declares that he has authority to search whether or not the person consents, the fact that the person offers no resistance does not indicate that he has consented. In one case, officers told a woman that they had a warrant to search her house. She replied, "Go ahead," and opened the door. It turned out that there either was no warrant at all or that the warrant was invalid. Holding that the search was unlawful, the Supreme Court said: "When a law enforcement officer claims authority to search a home under a warrant, he announces in effect that the occupant has no right to resist the search. The situation is instinct with coercion—albeit colorably lawful coercion. Where there is coercion there cannot be consent."[2]

It is not only an officer's threats or use of force or the display of authority that makes an expression of consent to a search ineffective. As in ordinary affairs, consent does not count if it is obtained by deceit. While an officer is not required to reveal everything about an investigation, ordinarily he cannot misrepresent the two critical facts that he is a police officer and that his purpose in requesting permission to enter is to conduct a search.* If the person asks specific questions and indicates that his willingness to permit a search depends on the answers, the officer must respond honestly. Since the person is free to give his consent to the search or to withhold it, an officer has no choice but to accept the person's judgment about what information is relevant to his decision.

In addition to avoiding actions of his own that would make consent ineffective, an officer should interpret cautiously the actions of the person whose consent he wants. The response to a request for consent will often be ambiguous, especially if the person has some fear of the police. Rather than assume that consent has been given, an officer should resolve an ambiguity by repeating his request or by stating his understanding of what has been said. Although no particular form of consent is required, it is always preferable that it be expressed explicitly. Rarely is it advisable to rely on actions alone or on silence in response to a request. An officer cannot always postpone a search until every detail is pinned down; but he acts unlawfully if he bases a search on consent that has not actually been given, and he risks that evidence found in the search will not be admissible in court.

An Appropriate Person

Most of the time, it is possible to tell from the circumstances whether a person has authority to consent to a search. If an adult answers the door of a private house, it is reasonable to assume that he is a regular occupant, unless there are indications to the contrary; and it would be reasonable to ask him for permission to search. A small child who came to the door would not be an appropriate person to consent to a search, nor would someone who was plainly a babysitter, or a casual guest, or a television repairman, even if there were no one else at home. It is always sensible to ask whether the person is the owner or occupant; and if there is any reason to suppose that he is not, it would be foolish not to ask.

*There is an exception to this general rule, which is discussed in Chapter 10 at pp. 127–128 below.

A person who gives consent does not have to be the owner of the premises. Authority to consent depends not on ownership but on use or the right to use. The person who consents must be someone who has regular, unconditional use of the premises. Commonly, more than one person meets that test. In a family home, for example, both husband and wife probably admit whom they choose; and, if so, either can consent to a search. If adult children live at home, they also may have the authority to consent; so also may the elderly parents of the husband or wife, if they live in the home and have regular, unlimited use of it. In cases of this kind, where persons use premises in common, the Supreme Court has said that authority to consent "rests...on mutual use of the property by persons generally having joint access or control for most purposes, so that it is reasonable to recognize that any of the co-inhabitants has the right to permit the inspection in his own right and that the others have assumed the risk that one of their number might permit the common area to be searched."[3]

Dwellings are shared not only by families but also by friends, roommates, and various kinds of groups living together temporarily or for long periods. Furthermore, there are many ways to subdivide a single dwelling unit. Persons may use a living room, kitchen, and bathroom in common, but each have his own bedroom, which the other does not ordinarily enter uninvited. Or a closet or a dresser may be used exclusively by one person, while the rest of the room is used in common. The variety of possible living arrangements is great, and often it is not readily apparent what the actual arrangement is. In each case, a person has authority to consent to a search of premises or a portion of premises that he shares with another person, if he ordinarily admits whomever he wishes to the place searched, without the permission of the other person.

One difficult situation that occurs with some frequency is a search of a child's room in his parents' house, when one or both of the parents consent to the search in the child's absence. No general rule easily resolves such cases, because the facts vary so much and are usually ambiguous about the privacies of the persons involved. If the house belongs to the parents, the child pays no rent, and the child uses the room as a member of the family rather than as an individual in his own right, it has usually been found that the parents have authority to consent to the search. Suppose, however, that the child is almost an adult and is largely independent, but that the parents own the house or pay the rent. In such a case, if there was an understanding that the room belonged to the child and that no one was to enter without his permission, a parent's consent would probably not be effective. Once the child is an adult or nearly an adult and no longer subject to the general supervision of his parents, it is usually wiser to treat him as an independent person despite the family relationship.

Up to this point, we have considered situations in which an officer asks for consent to search from an occupant who is present, while some other occupant is absent. Occasionally, several occupants are present, and consent is given by one and expressly withheld by another. That occurs rarely, since if joint occupants are getting along with one another, the objection of one will cause the other(s) to withhold consent also. If they do not agree and one of them has authority over the premises superior to the other, the decision of the former controls. A simple test is to ask whether the person who consents has authority to direct the one who objects to leave. If a homeowner and his guest are at the house when officers ask for permission to search, the owner's consent would prevail over the guest's objection; if the positions were reversed, the officers could not search over the owner's objection despite the permission of the guest. Of course, the owner's consent would not authorize the officers to search the guest's suitcase or similar containers that protected the privacy of the guest.

Suppose two persons have equal authority over the premises, one of whom consents to the search and the other does not; a husband and wife, for example, disagree about a search of the living room. Even if the consenting person persists despite the other's objection, a search in these circumstances is at best of doubtful validity. A firm answer is difficult to give because the general principle that authority to consent to a search depends on the ordinary understandings of the joint occupants breaks down; it is not clear what would happen if two occupants with equal authority disagreed about admitting some private person. In such a case, which is likely to arise very infrequently, it seems wise to follow a rule that a search *not* be undertaken without a search warrant.

It is not clear whether a search is lawful if an officer relies reasonably but mistakenly on the appearance that the person whose consent he obtains has authority to give it. Suppose, for example, that an officer asks for and obtains consent from a person who looks like the homeowner but who in fact is the television repairman. Some lower courts have concluded that as long as the officer has no reason to doubt the appearance of authority, a search based on apparent consent is lawful. The Supreme Court has not decided the question.[4] It makes sense to rely on appearances, so long as one is observant and pays attention to what the appearances actually are. If there is doubt that cannot be resolved, the preferable course is to obtain a search warrant.

While the rules discussed in this section may seem complex and hard to apply if all the possibilities are examined one after another, the general rule is straightforward and will usually provide an answer without difficulty: A person has authority to consent to a search to the extent that, in the conduct of ordinary affairs, he has authority in similar circumstances to admit someone without the permission of anyone else.

Consent Applicable to the Search

When authority to search depends on consent, the person who gives consent can impose whatever limits or conditions he chooses. He may give permission to search only certain rooms, only at certain times, or only for a limited period; having given consent, he can withdraw it at any time by communicating the withdrawal to the officer conducting the search. The officer may not like the restrictions. He may believe that they are pointless, or that they make it useless to search because the most likely place is excluded or because nothing is likely to be found in so short a time. Provided that he does not exert coercive pressure that renders an expression of consent ineffective, he can try to convince the person to modify or eliminate the restrictions. But he is otherwise bound to accept them. He does not have to agree to a restricted search; but if he does not, then he cannot justify the search on the basis of consent at all. He will then have to wait until he can obtain a warrant to search that does not have the same restrictions.

An explicit restriction—"Stay out of the bed-room!"—is easily understood and applied. Often, however, a person who gives permission to search will be less clear about his intentions; and later, he may assert that the officer ignored some restriction that was not so clear at the outset. If the consent was not in fact limited, the person cannot later claim that the search was unlawful; an officer who has permission does not search unlawfully. A conscientious officer will listen to the person's words and interpret them reasonably. If the person's intention is unclear, the officer should resolve it with a question. As in other situations, not only does such caution fulfill the responsibility of police to honor constitutional rights; it also increases the likelihood that a court will uphold the search if the person should later claim that the officer exceeded the permission he was given.

An officer who relies on consent as the basis for a search takes a certain risk. Even if he is careful and conscientious, there is a possibility that the person will later claim that the consent was not freely given or did not extend to the place where incriminating evidence was found, or that some other person against whom evidence is found will claim that consent was not obtained from the appropriate person. The risk is small in situations when the person plainly wants the officer to enter, like the householder who invites detectives to look around after a burglary. It is much larger when the officer is looking for evidence against the person on whose consent he relies or someone close to that person. An officer planning to conduct a search in those circumstances should consider whether it is practicable to obtain a search warrant. If not, reliance on consent may be unavoidable. The officer should then be alert to the risks and do what he can to avoid them. So long as he reasonably believes that he has been given appropriate consent for the search, he can proceed on that basis.

Questions for Discussion

1. Why is a search conducted with the permission of the occupant of the premises lawful?

2. What are the requirements for effective consent to a search?

3. Describe some common situations in which an officer might ask for consent to conduct a search.
   What factors in those situations would indicate that consent was given voluntarily?
   What factors would indicate that it was not given voluntarily?

4. What information must an officer give to a person from whom he seeks consent to a search?
   What other information should he give?

5. When there is more than one occupant or user of premises, what general rule determines whose consent is necessary and sufficient to authorize a search?
   Give some illustrations.

6. When two occupants have equal use of premises and one of them consents to a search, does it matter whether the other occupant is present (and objects to the search)?

Problem Cases

1. The police suspect that stolen goods are concealed in the basement of Thompson's house. An officer dressed as an employee of the electric company goes to the house and asks Mrs. Thompson if he can go to the basement to make an adjustment of the electricity meter. She gives her permission. While in the basement, the officer looks inside some cartons stacked near the meter and finds stolen goods. He continues to look around and finds narcotics that belong to Mrs. Thompson.

Is the search lawful?
Can the stolen goods be seized and used in evidence against Thompson and Mrs. Thompson?
Can the narcotics be seized and used in evidence against Mrs. Thompson?

2. Three generations of the White family live in one house. Mr. and Mrs. White, Senior share a bedroom and bathroom on the third floor. There is also a small sitting room on the third floor which they use most of the time but which is used as a guest room when a friend of anyone in the family sleeps at the house. Mr. and Mrs. John White share a master bedroom and bathroom on the second floor. They have two children: Mary, aged nineteen, and Robert, aged sixteen. Mary and Robert each have a bedroom on the second floor. They share a bathroom. On the first floor, there are a living room, dining room, kitchen, and a small television room. The house is owned by Mrs. John White; she makes the mortgage payments. The property tax is paid by Mr. John White. The police want to search the White house.

Whose consent is necessary to search the various parts of the house? Consider the situation (1) when other members of the household are present, and (2) when other members of the household are absent. If you do not have enough information, what further information would enable you to answer?

3. Police officers went to the home of Mrs. Howe and informed her that they had a warrant to search the house. She said, "Go ahead and search," and opened the door. During the search, which lasted for some time, Mrs. Howe made no objection. On several occasions, she opened drawers or closets for the officers. The officers had no warrant.

Was the search lawful?

Notes

1. Schneckloth v. Bustamonte, 412 U.S. 218, 220 (1973).
2. Bumper v. North Carolina, 391 U.S. 543, 550 (1968).
3. United States v. Matlock, 415 U.S. 164, 171 n.7 (1974).
4. In United States v. Matlock, 415 U.S. 164, 177 n.14 (1974), the Supreme Court raised but declined to answer the question. For a lower court's opinion upholding the search, see, e.g., United States v. Sells, 496 F.2d 912 (7th Cir. 1974).

CHAPTER 10

EAVESDROPPING, WIRETAPPING, AND SECRET SURVEILLANCE

Police officers do not have much occasion to undertake deliberate eavesdropping in the course of their ordinary duties. They are even less likely to engage in electronic eavesdropping and wiretapping, which require sophisticated equipment and careful planning in advance. These specialized investigative techniques are used mostly in cases of unusual importance, which merit the commitment of time and resources. Despite the infrequent use of electronic devices, the development of increasingly sophisticated technology has caused wide public concern about their potential misuse. Officers should be informed about the subject even if they are unlikely themselves to face problems in this area.

This chapter discusses the principles of constitutional law that have to do with eavesdropping and wiretapping. In addition, extensive federal and state legislation regulates the use of electronic or mechanical devices to overhear or intercept conversations.[1] An officer who contemplates using such a device has to be familiar with all of the applicable laws. Rarely, if ever, would an officer employ a device without following standard departmental procedures and obtaining the explicit approval of headquarters.

General Principles

The constitutional approach to eavesdropping and interception of conversations treats a person's oral communication as "effects," which the Fourth Amendment protects against unreasonable search and seizure. We do not usually think of someone who secretly listens to a conversation as conducting a search, nor do we think of the words he hears as having been seized. But it is easy to understand how those concepts are used. Just as the Fourth Amendment prohibits an unreasonable physical invasion of privacy to seize tangible goods, it also prohibits an unreasonable invasion of privacy to hear what is expected to be a private conversation.

In the same way that an officer who is lawfully where he is can observe his surroundings and, if he comes across evidence of a crime, seize it, he can listen to conversations going on around him and, if he hears evidence of a crime, "seize" it—that is, use it in any appropriate way in the performance of his duties or remember it and later testify about what he heard. An officer on patrol violates no one's rights if he overhears two people negotiating a narcotics transaction on the street or near an open window inside a house. If they speak so loudly that the officer hears them, it does not matter that they did not want to be overheard and thought that they were not. So long as the officer is allowed to be where he is—in a public place or with authorization in a private place—and does not take special steps to hear what would ordinarily not be overheard,* he has not violated the Fourth Amendment.

The use of an electronic or other device to hear what would otherwise be unheard is governed by the preceding analysis. Such a device violates the reasonable expectation of privacy of a person who is unaware that a device is being used.

Katz v. United States

FBI agents had strong grounds for belief that Katz was using a telephone booth to transmit gambling information interstate, in violation of federal law. His past behavior

---

*When a conversation takes place on the street or in a similar public place, it is not clear whether eavesdropping by means of a special device is prohibited by the Fourth Amendment. It seems clear, at least, that the Fourth Amendment does not prohibit an officer from listening to such a conversation surreptitiously without a device, either in disguise or from a place of concealment.

indicated that he made the illegal calls at the same time each day, from the same booth. The agents placed an electronic listening and recording device on the outside of the booth. In this way, they obtained recordings of six short conversations between Katz and another person. Katz was later prosecuted, and the conversations were used in evidence against him.[2]

The Supreme Court declared that the agents' actions were not permitted by the Constitution. "The Government's activities in electronically listening to and recording...[Katz's] words violated the privacy upon which he justifiably relied while using the telephone booth and thus constituted a 'search and seizure' within the meaning of the Fourth Amendment."[3] When Katz entered the telephone booth and closed the door, he was entitled to assume that he was not being overheard. This was so, even though the walls of the booth were made of glass. He could not have expected to remain unseen while he was in the booth, but he could reasonably expect that his words were unheard.

The Constitution prohibits only those searches and seizures that are unreasonable. In *Katz*, the Government argued that the eavesdropping was reasonable because the agents had probable cause to believe that Katz was making illegal use of the telephone and they listened to and recorded only the conversations believed to be illegal. The Supreme Court agreed that in those circumstances electronic eavesdropping might be reasonable; even so, it was lawful only if the agents had obtained prior judicial authorization, like a search warrant. The Court treated electronic eavesdropping like any other planned search, to which none of the special rules allowing a warrantless search applies. Therefore, the eavesdropping without a warrant was unlawful.

There are several lessons of the *Katz* case. First, it cannot be argued that eavesdropping or wiretapping does not violate the Fourth Amendment simply because it is conducted without a physical entry or trespass on private property. In *Katz*, the electronic device was attached to the outside of the telephone booth; the absence of an entry into the booth while Katz was inside made no difference. Second, the Fourth Amendment does not prohibit all electronic eavesdropping. If the requirement of probable cause is met and if the use of the device is reasonably restricted to avoid unnecessarily hearing irrelevant private conversations, the eavesdropping falls within the Amendment's allowance of a reasonable search and seizure. Third, since any use of such a device requires planning in advance and since none of the special reasons for allowing a search without a warrant is applicable, electronic eavesdropping must always be authorized by a judicial order. Federal and state legislation provide in detail how such an order is obtained.

Further Applications

Additional applications of technology to law enforcement present issues like those raised by electronic eavesdropping and interception of conversations. A variety of devices can be used to obtain evidence that otherwise could not be obtained without an invasion of privacy prohibited by the Fourth Amendment. For example, a device for amplifying sounds might enable an officer on the street to hear a conversation in a private house. Or an officer might use binoculars to see something on private premises not visible to the naked eye. Electronic tracking devices enable investigators to monitor the location of movable items even though they are removed to a private place. Sometimes an officer can accomplish surreptitious surveillance of a private place by unusual efforts that do not require a device. Knowing that criminal suspects are in a motel unit, an officer might enter the adjoining unit and hear a conversation by lying on the floor near a locked door between the units.

In such cases, the constitutional test is whether the officer's action, with or without a special device, violated a *legitimate expectation of privacy*. We have seen that an officer who is allowed to be where he is can lawfully overhear or see what goes on audibly and visibly around him. But if he uses highly unusual methods against which ordinary caution does not guard to penetrate a private place, the fact that he has not invaded it physically does not render the Fourth Amendment inapplicable. As in *Katz*, the test is whether the method used invaded privacy on which the person observed justifiably relied. If so, the requirements of the Fourth Amendment must be met.

Eavesdropping with the Consent of a Party

When the agents placed the eavesdropping device on the outside of Katz's telephone booth, they did not have the permission either of Katz or of the person to whom he was talking. Sometimes officers are able to work with an undercover agent or an informer, who agrees to have a conversation with a criminal suspect that is transmitted or recorded. The device may be concealed on the agent or in the place where the conversation is held. In such circumstances, the principles discussed in connection with the *Katz* case do not apply.

If one of the parties to the conversation has agreed to the use of an eavesdropping or recording device, it can be argued that the other parties are in the same position as if he were simply to report the whole conversation to the police. While they may expect the conversation to remain private, their expectation is based on their misplaced confidence in the person with whom they talk. Since the Fourth Amendment does not prohibit a person from revealing what was said in a private conversation, it does not prohibit him from transmitting it directly or recording it without the knowledge of the others. The Supreme Court has observed: "If the law gives no protection to the wrongdoer whose trusted accomplice is or becomes a police agent, neither should it protect him when that same agent has recorded or transmitted the conversations which are later offered in evidence to prove the State's case."[4]

This reasoning was applied by the Court to conversations between a "wired informer" and another person in the informer's home and car, the other person's home, and a restaurant.[5] The variety of locations indicates that when one of the parties to a conversation has consented to secret eavesdropping, the location of the conversation is immaterial (provided, of course, that there is no violation of the Fourth Amendment aside from the eavesdropping).*

Undercover Agents

As the preceding discussion indicates, the use of an undercover agent, someone working for the government who pretends not to be, to obtain evidence of crime is not prohibited. In every large city, officers posing as purchasers obtain evidence against narcotics dealers. Without such subterfuge, it would be difficult to apprehend and convict persons who commit "victimless" crimes like narcotics offenses. If the acts of an undercover agent independent of the deception are permissible, the deception itself, by which the agent gains the confidence of the criminal, violates no constitutional right.

In Chapter 9, we noted that an officer does not need a search warrant to enter and search private premises if he has appropriate consent. We noted further that consent must not be obtained by force or threat or, ordinarily, by deceiving the person whose consent is sought about the purpose of the entry. However, the Supreme Court has held that if an undercover agent is invited into private premises for an express purpose and does only that for which he was invited to enter, without making any search, there is no violation of the Fourth Amendment.

Lewis v. United States

"On December 3...Edward Cass, an undercover federal narcotics agent, telephoned petitioner's [Lewis's] home to inquire about the possibility of purchasing marihuana. Cass, who previously had not met or dealt with petitioner, falsely identified himself as one 'Jimmy the Pollack [sic]' and stated that a mutual friend had told

*Once a criminal prosecution has begun, the constitutional right to the assistance of counsel prohibits surreptitious listening to conversations of the defendant. See pp. 173–176 below.

him petitioner might be able to supply marihuana. In response, petitioner said, 'Yes. I believe, Jimmy, I can take care of you,' and directed Cass to his home where, it was indicated a sale of marihuana would occur. Cass drove to petitioner's home, knocked on the door, identified himself as 'Jim,' and was admitted. After discussing the possibility of regular future dealings at a discounted price, petitioner led Cass to a package located on the front porch of his home. Cass gave petitioner $50, took the package, and left the premises. The package contained five bags of marihuana. On December 17...a similar transaction took place, beginning with a phone conversation in which Cass identified himself as 'Jimmy the Pollack' and ending with an invited visit by Cass to petitioner's home where a second sale of marihuana occurred. Once again, Cass paid petitioner $50, but this time he received in return a package containing six bags of marihuana."[6]

The Supreme Court held that Cass's entries into Lewis's home were lawful and that he could testify about them at Lewis's trial for narcotics offenses. Had Cass sought to accomplish any purpose other than the transaction for which he was admitted, the entry would have been without consent and unlawful. When there is doubt about what will occur, an officer who expects to enter a private place on the basis of consent obtained by subterfuge is well-advised to obtain a warrant, if that is practicable. In *Lewis*, all doubt about the outcome would have been avoided had the agent, having probable cause to believe that a narcotics transaction would take place, obtained a warrant to enter Lewis's house for the purpose of the transaction.

Occasional Police Agents

Officers investigating a crime sometimes are able to enlist the temporary aid of a person who is in a specially favorable position to obtain evidence. Although there is no restriction on the use of evidence that a private person turns over to the police on his own initiative, officers need to be mindful of constitutional requirements if they ask a private person to do something that he would not have done independently. Wanting to search a hotel room, for example, and lacking probable cause to obtain a search warrant, officers might ask a chambermaid to look for specific items when she cleans the room. If she departs from her normal cleaning activities to look for the items, her conduct is no more lawful than a search by the officers themselves would have been. Since she is acting for them and at their request, she is considered to be their agent, to whom the restrictions of the Fourth Amendment apply. It makes no difference whether she is asked to do a great deal or very little, once or repeatedly, for pay or not. The critical fact is that the police have induced her to do something for them that they could not lawfully have done themselves.

It is not always easy to distinguish a private person's independent assistance from the solicited assistance of an agent. If a chambermaid finds money under a mattress when she is making a bed and turns it over to the police because she thinks it might be stolen, she acts as a private person and no constitutional question is raised. But suppose she finds the money after detectives investigating a bank robbery have told her that they suspect one of the hotel guests and have asked her to "keep her eyes open." If the admission of the money in evidence is challenged, the judge will have to assess all the circumstances and make a difficult decision about whether the chambermaid's conduct was more like that of a private person or more like that of an officer acting without a warrant. Officers seeking cooperation from private persons must observe a line separating actions that they initiate from the receipt of evidence or information from a private person acting on his own.*

Entrapment

Important as it is to investigate crime and to prosecute and convict criminals, no one will approve an investigative practice that leads someone to commit a crime that he otherwise would not have committed. An undercover

*See the discussion of United States v. Henry, p. 175 below.

agent in contact with someone whom he suspects of criminal activity should avoid any conduct that might incite and persuade the person to commit a crime that he has no independent disposition to commit. It would be far better for the agent to conclude that his suspicion was unfounded than for him to encourage the commission of a crime by his persistence.

If that should occur, the law recognizes a defense called entrapment. The defense is not available to someone who is ready and willing to commit a crime, for whom the government's agent merely furnishes an opportunity. In *Lewis*, for example, the undercover agent furnished an opportunity for a sale of marijuana that Lewis was all too ready to make. Entrapment is a defense against criminal charges if the government agent instigated the crime, that is if he put the idea of committing the crime in the person's head and lured him to commit it.

The line between providing an opportunity for a crime and instigating it is not always easy to draw. An undercover agent engaged in solitary contacts with a suspected criminal may find it particularly difficult to observe that distinction. Many people believe that government agents in the role of undercover investigators should not become actively involved in a criminal enterprise, even if they do not actually instigate the crime.[7] Although the law does not presently reflect that view, a court may dismiss a prosecution if it finds that the government participated too extensively in the commission of the crime. An officer working in an undercover capacity should constantly question his suspicions; if there is a fair chance that without his involvement the crime will not be committed, he should withdraw.

Questions for Discussion

1. What provision of the Constitution applies to eavesdropping and secret interception of oral communications? Explain the reasoning by which that provision is applied.

2. In what circumstances might an officer overhear a private conversation without raising any constitutional issue? Why is that so?

3. In what circumstances is the use of an electronic or other device to overhear a private conversation permitted?

4. Does it make any difference if a party to a private conversation has secretly given his permission for a government agent to listen by means of a concealed device?

5. What provisions of the law of your state are applicable to the use of electronic or other listening and recording devices?

6. What regulations and procedures are followed in your department to obtain authorization for the use of a listening or recording device?

7. In what circumstances can a government agent enter private premises to obtain evidence of crime without revealing his identity or the purpose of his entry?

8. If an officer can accept evidence of a crime from a private person who was a witness, why can he not ask a private person to enter private premises to look for evidence?

9. What is entrapment? Why is it prohibited?

Problem Cases

1. Officers obtained a warrant to search Black's house for narcotics. They searched while no one was at home. After they found and seized a quantity of narcotics, they planted a secret transmitting device in Black's living room. The next day, by means of the device, they overheard an incriminating conversation between Black and a confederate in Black's living room.

Was the conversation overheard lawfully?

2. Officer Rand posed as a user of narcotics and made several street transactions. After he had made contact with a large dealer, he hid a transmitter under his clothing and engaged in conversations with the dealer on the street, in a restaurant, in Rand's car, in the dealer's car, and in the dealer's home. At the start of each conversation, the dealer said something like, "Talk low, I don't want to take any chance that this will be overheard by a bug or something," to which

Rand responded, "Stop worrying. No one's listening." All of the conversations were transmitted and overheard by other officers.

Were the conversations overheard lawfully?

3. Foster, a detective on the robbery squad, made contact with Stace, who was a receiver of stolen goods. Pretending to be interested in making a purchase, Foster arranged to meet Stace at Stace's house. While he was at the house, Foster bought two stolen cameras. Stace also showed him stolen phonographs, which Foster did not buy. Foster saw in a pile in the corner a number of fur coats, which Stace told him were also stolen goods and for sale. Just before Foster left the house, Stace received a telephone call. Foster heard him say to the person on the telephone that he had a lot of hot goods, which he would be willing to sell if the price were right.

How much of what Foster saw and heard at Stace's house is admissible in evidence against Stace?

Notes

1. The federal legislation is contained in 18 U.S.C. §§2510–20.
2. Katz v. United States, 389 U.S. 347 (1967).
3. *Id.* at 353.
4. United States v. White, 401 U.S. 745, 752 (1971).
5. United States v. White, *supra* note 4.
6. Lewis v. United States, 385 U.S. 206, 207–208 (1966) (footnotes omitted).
7. See, for example, the dissenting opinion of Justice Brennan in Hampton v. United States, 425 U.S. 484, 495 (1976); the dissenting opinions of Justice Douglas and Justice Stewart in United States v. Russell, 411 U.S. 423, 436, 439 (1973); the opinion of Justice Frankfurter concurring in the result in Sherman v. United States, 356 U.S. 369, 378 (1958); and the separate opinion of Justice Roberts in Sorrells v. United States, 287 U.S. 435, 453 (1932).

CHAPTER 11

THE STATION: BOOKING AND PHYSICAL EXAMINATIONS

Unlike most of the peace-keeping and investigative functions that we have considered, the work that police perform at the police station after an arrest can usually be planned in advance. The applicable constitutional principles reflect this difference between an unplanned street

BOSTON POLICE DEPARTMENT
ARREST BOOKING SHEET

01. District		02. Cell No.

03. Booking Number	04. Complaint No.	05. Central Records No.	06. Date	07. Arrest Time	☐ A ☐ P

08. Booking Charges

09. Location of Arrest | 10. Additional Clearances (CC Numbers)

ARRESTEE

11. Name (Last, First, MI)	12. Address

13. Alias	14. Sex ☐ M ☐ F	15. Race	16. Age	17. DOB	18. Place of Birth

19. Parents' First Names	20. Mother's Maiden Name	21. Wife's Full Maiden Name	22. Husband's First Name

23. Height	24. Weight	25. Hair	26. Eyes	27. Build	28. Complexion	29. Marital ☐ Marr. ☐ Unmarr.	30. Occupation	31. Soc. Sec. No.

32. Scars, Marks, Other Descriptive Data	Op. License No.

CONTROL

33. Arrested With: (Booking Numbers and Names) #1 #2	34. Others ☐ Yes (See Incid. Rpt.) ☐ No

35. Arresting Officer	36. Unit of Arrest. Off.	37. ID No.	38. Partner's ID

39. Transported By (Unit):	40. Booking Officer Signature	41. ID No.	42. Time ☐ A ☐ P

43. Searched By:	44. ID No.	45. Placed in Cell By:	46. ID No.

47. Arrest Process ☐ No Warrant ☐ Summons Warrant No. Court

48. I was informed of my right to remain silent, to use a phone, to call a lawyer, or to have one provided for me. Signature	49. Phone Used ☐ Yes ☐ No

50. Informed of Rights By: Signature	51. ID No.	52. Time ☐ A ☐ P

53. Visible Injuries: Examined at Hospital ☐ Yes ☐ No | 54. Property Other: | Money: $

55. Vehicle (Reg. State, Number) | 56. Disposition

Signature of Prisoner

ID

57. ID Process ☐ Yes ☐ No	58. Photo No.	59. Teletype No.	60. Breathalyzer ☐ Yes ☐ No	61. Wanted ☐ Yes ☐ No	62. Warrant No.	Court/Jurisdiction	63. ID of Notifying Off.

JUVENILE

64. Person Notified	65. Relationship	66. Address	67. Phone	68. Date	69. Time ☐ A ☐ P

70. Notified By:	71. ID No.	72. Name of Juv. Prob. Officer	73. Juvenile Paroled To:

74. Additional Information

OUT

75. Prisoner Transferred To:	76. Pris. Prop. Received By:	77. ID No.	78. I Received Property Listed Under Item 54. Signature

79. Bail Set By:	80. Bailed By:	81. Amount	82. I Selected Bail Comm. Signature	83. Date/Time Released ☐ A ☐ P

COURT

84. Court Charges (Major Charge First)	85. Code	86. Disposition	87. Court	88. Date in Court

HEADQUARTERS RECORDS

encounter and operations at the station. Constitutional rights are protected on the street as elsewhere; but the law takes account of the difficulties of law enforcement in a sudden, threatening situation. When the scene shifts to the police station, the urgencies of time and place are relaxed, and it is appropriate to require careful and explicit attention to the rights of the arrested person.

In this chapter, we shall consider the practice of booking and the general principles that apply to investigative techniques at the station. The procedures for identification lineups and for questioning arrested persons raise special constitutional issues and are discussed in the next two chapters.

Booking

The collection of statistics and general information about crime within the jurisdiction is an accepted part of police work. Central to this enterprise is the compilation of

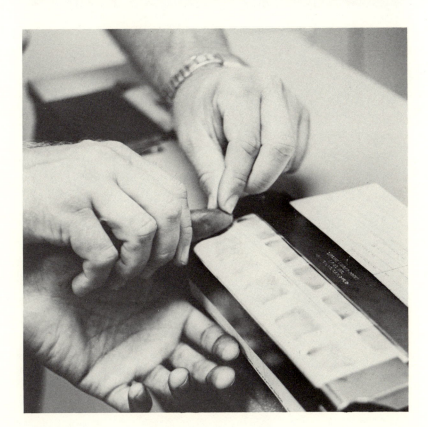

Figure 11-1.
Arrest Booking Sheet
[Opposite]

arrest records, which contain information about persons who are arrested and brought to the police station: identifying physical characteristics and items of public record or generally available personal data, like address, date of birth, employment, and social security number. In addition, booking typically includes fingerprinting and photographing. The information, including fingerprints and photograph, is placed on a standard form, a copy of which is usually sent to the FBI for its permanent national file. Most people regard booking as part of the arrest itself. There is little dispute that having made a lawful arrest, police have authority to collect and record this kind of nonprivate, identifying information.

Although arrested persons usually cooperate and booking procedures are carried out without incident, police do not have authority to *require* a person to answer their questions or to submit to being fingerprinted and photographed. Nor does their authority allow them to *force* a person to cooperate. If someone refuses to give information or to be fingerprinted or photographed, that fact may be noted on the arrest report. It may have a bearing on a magistrate's decision about temporary detention or the conditions of bail or on subsequent proceedings by the prosecution, which lie beyond the responsibility of the police.

The arresting officer and officers involved in the booking process should keep in mind that the person being booked has not yet been convicted or, usually, even formally accused of any crime, however certain the appearance of guilt. There is no basis for any kind of punitive action at the police station. An arrested person is

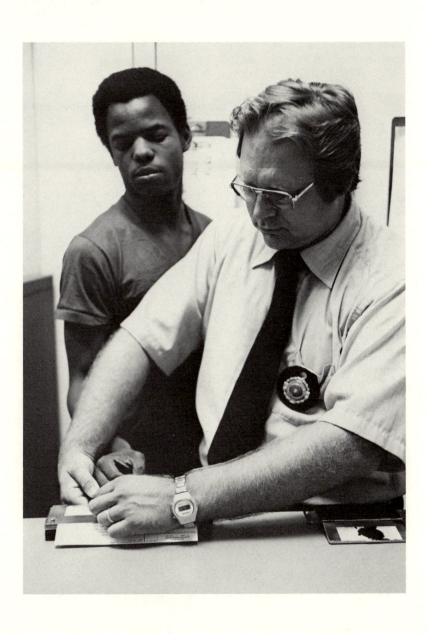

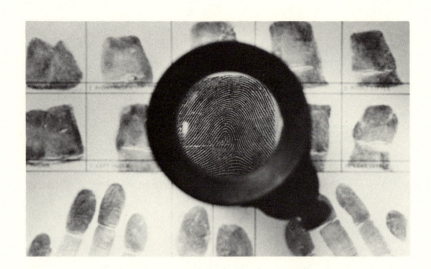

Figure 11-2a.
Fingerprint and
Identification Card
(Front)

IDENTIFICATION SECTION · POLICE DEPARTMENT, BOSTON, MASS.

MALE

Name_____

Alias_____

Photo No._____ Crim. Record No._____

Prints taken by_____ Date_____

At_____

Classified by_____

F. P. FORMULA

1. RIGHT THUMB	2. RIGHT INDEX	3. RIGHT MIDDLE	4. RIGHT RING	5. RIGHT LITTLE

6. LEFT THUMB	7. LEFT INDEX	8. LEFT MIDDLE	9. LEFT RING	10. LEFT LITTLE

FOUR LEFT FINGERS	FOUR RIGHT FINGERS

entitled to the same respect from public officials that accompanies performance of ordinary police duties and as much liberty as is consistent with the arrest itself. In the aftermath of an apparently criminal and possibly dangerous situation, officers are not expected to display much affection for the person whom they have arrested. Nevertheless, it is not unrealistic to ask that they act with deliberation and conscious regard for his rights and dignity. Strict observance of the arrested person's rights throughout the process of arrest is the mark of professional police work and the best means of insuring that evidence useful to the prosecution is not inadvertently rendered inadmissible because of failure to comply with constitutional requirements.

Figure 11-2b.
Fingerprint and Identification Card (Back)

Form 1062.

Age	years	Compl.		Beard		MARKS AND PECULIARITIES
Date of Birth		Height		Eyes		
Birthplace		Weight		Nose		
Descent		Build		Occupation		
Color		Hair				

Arrested by			District	Date
Offence		Disposition	Court	Date

CRIMINAL RECORD

NAME	DATE	OFFENCE	PLACE AND COURT	SENTENCE

BOTH THUMBS, TAKEN TOGETHER

Remarks

Signature

Residence

Examinations and Tests

Police have authority to carry out ordinary examinations and tests with the cooperation of an arrested person. So long as such procedures have a serious investigative purpose, police need no authorization beyond the arrest itself to direct the person to cooperate, in the same way that they take his fingerprints and photograph him during booking. Procedures appropriate to a particular case depend on the crime and the evidence already recovered. In addition to fingerprints and the lineup and questioning procedures considered below, in special cases, investigators may have reason to obtain a sample of hair, blood, or urine; scrapings from under fingernails; or a handwriting sample.*

Whenever a sample is to be taken from a person's body, the constitutional guarantee of due process of law as well as standards of ordinary decency require the use of safe, hygienic methods. Officers should assure the person of this and explain in advance what will be done. Special care should be taken to avoid abusive physical contact and to cause neither pain nor embarrassment. In a few unusual cases, authority has been sought to perform a minor surgical procedure to recover an object, typically a bullet, lodged beneath the skin. Such cases have involved an exchange of gunfire, in which the intended victim of the crime or a police officer believes he hit the criminal; the bullet is sought as evidence to connect the person with the crime. Courts have authorized such a procedure very rarely, and only when the procedure involves minimal risk and little pain or inconvenience. In no case should police officials attempt to perform any such technique, which is authorized if at all subject to the strictest safeguards of the person's health and safety.

An arrested person sometimes refuses to cooperate and resists even efforts that require only his passive cooperation. Officers should not use physical force to carry out a procedure, even if it may materially aid their investigation. On one or two occasions, a court has suggested that officers are allowed to use physical force if it is necessary to obtain a person's cooperation in an

*The Fifth Amendment's privilege against compulsory self-incrimination does not prohibit such procedures. See p. 144 below.

authorized procedure.[1] Taking note of those rulings, one cannot say that the matter is free from doubt. On the other side of the issue, the Supreme Court has held that officers' use of extreme physical abuse to recover pills that an arrested person had swallowed at the moment of arrest was conduct that "shocks the conscience," which the Constitution does not permit.[2]

Judicial rulings are not necessary for us to conclude that officers should not, on their own initiative, use physical force against a person to carry out an investigative procedure. Almost always it will be practicable to postpone action until a judicial order expressly authorizing the procedure has been obtained; a refusal to comply with the order is a contempt of court with which the court itself can deal. Even if postponement may make the procedure useless—for example, if a test for the alcoholic content of blood is too long delayed—a person's failure to cooperate with a proper procedure is ordinarily admissible in evidence, and the jury or judge is likely to infer that the results of the procedure would have been unfavorable to him.

If it is kept in mind that the purpose of investigative procedures is to obtain evidence in aid of prosecution and that they have no independent value of their own, it will not appear preferable to force compliance rather than resort to the court for enforcement. The use of force needlessly casts a shadow over the evidence obtained, however reliable it is in fact. It also raises the possibility of a countercharge of excessive force against the police, which, even if it has no bearing on the defendant's guilt or innocence, brings discredit on the police and on the government generally.

Post-arrest procedures at the stationhouse may seem an unlikely occasion for emphasis on individual rights. The person involved is thought to be guilty of a crime that justifies taking him into custody. In some cases, he will have resisted the arrest and endangered officers and others. The police station, however, is the single location where officers can fully control the circumstances of their work. Their clear adherence to the highest standards of professional conduct there will encourage respect for their larger role in the community.

Questions for Discussion

1. How does police work performed on the street differ from work done at the station?
   What is the significance of the difference?

2. Examine the form used by your department to record information about a person who has been arrested.
   What information is included?
   In what circumstances would the various items of information be valuable for police work?

3. What provision is made in your department for the performance of special tests and examinations of an arrested person?
   What regulations affect the manner in which such procedures are to be carried out?

Notes

1. See, e.g., United States v. Cunningham, 509 F.2d 961 (D.C. Cir. 1975).
2. Rochin v. California, 342 U.S. 165 (1952).

CHAPTER 12

LINEUPS

This chapter discusses the constitutional principles that apply to procedures for the identification of criminal suspects. The use of lineups and similar techniques for witnesses to identify a suspect is well-established. The value of direct testimony of an eyewitness as proof of guilt is recognized by prosecutors and defense counsel alike. At the same time, all recognize that such evidence, which depends entirely on the witness's perception and judgment, is subject to peculiar risks of mistake. Courts have sought to develop principles that permit identifications under appropriate safeguards, without risk that an innocent person will be incriminated mistakenly.

In an ordinary lineup the suspect appears with four or five other persons roughly matching the witness's description of the criminal. The persons in the lineup may be asked to put on an article of clothing, to make gestures or movements, or to repeat words like those that the witness recalls. On rare occasions, if a witness did not see the criminal but heard his voice, there may be a "voice lineup," in which the witness listens to a number of different voices. A suspect may be required to make any reasonable display of physical characteristics, including his voice, if the display may facilitate an identification and does not harass or unduly embarrass or impose on him.

The particular techniques that are used vary widely from one police department to another. Departments of large cities may have access to technology, such as videotapes, that would be too costly for departments in smaller communities. All, however, are subject to the same requirements of constitutional law.

The Fourth and Fifth Amendments

In Chapter 11, we noted that a lawful arrest gives the police authority to carry out investigative procedures at the station during the brief period before the person is taken before a judicial official. That rule includes identification procedures like lineups. Except for the authority to arrest, based on probable cause, police have no authority to take someone into custody in order to conduct a lineup. Similarly, once their custody of a person has ended, they cannot take him into custody a second time solely for a lineup. That would constitute a separate seizure of the person, prohibited by the Fourth Amendment unless it were done pursuant to a judicial order. If a person is detained by the magistrate instead of being released on bail, it may be possible to arrange a lineup while he is in detention. In most cases, however, a lineup occurs during the period of initial custody following an arrest.

We shall discuss the scope of the Fifth Amendment privilege against self-incrimination in the next chapter. We noted in Chapter 11 that physical examinations and tests are permitted even though incriminating evidence, like a blood or hair sample, may be taken from a suspect. The same is true of lineups. The privilege is not violated so long as the person must only display himself and his identifying physical characteristics and is not asked to affirm or deny the truth of any incriminating statement.

After Formal Criminal Proceedings Begin: The Assistance of Counsel

The Sixth Amendment provides that a person accused of a crime shall have "the assistance of counsel for his defense." A person has the right to be assisted by defense counsel at a lineup conducted after "the initiation of adversary judicial proceedings''[1] against him—that is, after he has been formally accused of a crime (by indictment or information) or been brought before a judicial official for a statement of the charges against him and a hearing.

United States v. Wade

"The federally insured bank in Eustace, Texas, was robbed on September 21....A man with a small strip of tape on each side of his face entered the bank, pointed a pistol at the female cashier and the vice president, the only persons in the bank at the time, and forced them to fill a pillowcase with the bank's money. The man then drove away with an accomplice who had been waiting in a stolen car outside the bank. On March 23...an indictment was returned against...Wade, and two others for conspiring to rob the bank, and against Wade and the accomplice for the robbery itself. Wade was arrested on April 2, and counsel was appointed to represent him on April 26. Fifteen days later an FBI agent, without notice to Wade's lawyer, arranged to have the two bank employees observe a lineup made up of Wade and five or six other prisoners and conducted in a courtroom of the local county courthouse. Each person in the line wore strips of tape such as allegedly worn by the robber and upon direction each said something like 'put the money in the bag,' the words allegedly uttered by the robber. Both bank employees identified Wade in the lineup as the bank robber.

"At trial, the two employees, when asked on direct examination if the robber was in the courtroom, pointed to Wade. The prior lineup identification was then elicited from both employees on cross-examination."[2]

Wade's lawyer argued that the witnesses' identification of Wade in the courtroom violated his Sixth Amendment right to counsel, because their identifications depended on the previous lineup at which his lawyer was not present. The Supreme Court agreed. It held that unless other measures are taken to guard against a mistaken identification, the presence of counsel at a lineup such as Wade's is constitutionally required. Otherwise, it said, the defendant's ability to defend himself at trial might be irreparably impaired.

The opinion in *Wade* discusses the dangers of mistaken identifications at length. The Court observed: "The vagaries of eyewitness identification are well-known; the annals of criminal law are rife with instances of mistaken identification."[3] Furthermore, a large factor contributing to mistakes is the suggestiveness of lineup procedures, which too often indicate to a witness which person the police expect him to identify. Having made an identification at a lineup, the witness almost always identifies the same person at the trial. The critical identification is usually the first.

The Court concluded that the presence of the accused's lawyer at a pretrial lineup would protect against the danger of mistake in two ways. First, the lawyer's presence would encourage police to conduct a lineup fairly and reliably. Secondly, having observed how the lineup was conducted, the lawyer would be able at trial to bring out any indications of unfairness or suggestiveness, which the jury or judge could take into account. A lawyer would be better able than the accused himself to recognize dangers of mistake and expose them. Other kinds of evidence are also obtained in the absence of defense counsel; but ordinary trial techniques like cross-examination are adequate to test its accuracy. The peculiar risks of a lineup and the difficulty of exposing them at trial, as well as the weight likely to be given to an eyewitness identification, led the Court to regard lineups as distinct.

The opinion in *Wade* does not declare flatly that a lineup conducted without an opportunity for defense counsel to be present is unlawful. A lineup can be conducted without counsel if alternative measures are taken to "eliminate the risks of abuse and unintentional suggestion at lineup proceedings and the impediments to meaningful confrontation at trial."[4] Local police departments can devise their own practices, which might include videotaping a lineup, promulgation of detailed regulations specifying how lineups should be conducted and regular intradepartmental supervision of lineups, or the presence at a lineup of a legally trained person to perform counsel's task. The method used must give reasonable assurance of reliability and provide a basis for review and challenge by defense counsel.

Although the police are required (unless an adequate alternative is used) to give defense counsel an opportunity to appear at a reasonable time and place, they are not responsible for his presence. They have no authority to require him to appear and can proceed without him if he does not. Furthermore, the lawyer's role is that of an observer, not a participant. If the lawyer makes suggestions for improving the reliability of the lineup, the officer in charge should consider them carefully and accept them if they are reasonable and practicable. All such suggestions and, if they are rejected, the reasons for rejecting them should be recorded. Sometimes officers have allowed the lawyer to observe only the lineup itself and not the witness's identification or their interviews with the witness before or after the lineup. Since exchanges between officers and the witness and the witness's manner of making an identification may have a bearing on its reliability, a lawyer should ordinarily be allowed to be present when these events take place, provided that he does not interfere with the officer's work. The police can have no interest in an unfair or unreliable procedure. They lose nothing by allowing a lineup to be observed fully, and the prosecution gains a good deal of credibility.

If counsel is not given an opportunity to observe and there is no adequate alternative, the usual rule excluding evidence obtained in violation of constitutional rights applies; testimony about any identification made at the lineup is excluded from the defendant's trial. And since the lineup identification is often the critical one, a courtroom identification after an improper lineup is not permitted either, unless the government can show "by clear and convincing evidence"[5] that it is independent of the prior lineup, a difficult test to meet. Officers conducing a lineup after criminal proceedings have begun should be careful to comply with *Wade* not only for the primary reason that they will minimize the risk of mistaken identification but also because they will avoid the exclusion of eyewitness testimony indicative of guilt.

Before Formal Criminal Proceedings Begin: Due Process of Law

Wade had already been indicted by a grand jury when he was arrested, for a bank robbery that had occurred six months before. The lineup was held more than a month after his arrest and two weeks after a lawyer had been appointed to defend him, while he was being detained pending trial. In those circumstances, there would have been no delay or difficulty if the officers who arranged the lineup had notified Wade's lawyer. More commonly, however, an arrest follows soon after the crime itself, before any formal step toward prosecution has been taken or the person arrested has a lawyer. In those circumstances, the police do not have to postpone a lineup until defense counsel is available. While they are required to conduct a lineup fairly and reliably, the Sixth Amendment's specific guarantee of the right to counsel does not apply.

Kirby v. Illinois

"On February 21...a man named Willie Shard reported to the Chicago police that the previous day two men had robbed him on a Chicago street of a wallet containing, among other things, traveler's checks and a Social Security card. On February 22, two police officers stopped the petitioner [Kirby] and a companion, Ralph Bean, on West Madison Street in Chicago. When asked for identification, the petitioner produced a wallet that contained three traveler's checks and a Social Security card, all bearing the name of Willie Shard. Papers with Shard's name on them were also found in Bean's possession. When asked to explain his possession of Shard's property, the petitioner first said that the traveler's checks were 'play money,' and then told the officers that he had won them in a crap game. The officers then arrested the petitioner and Bean and took them to a police station.[*]

[*]The lawfulness of the stop and arrest was not in issue. If they had been unlawful, the items belonging to Shard on Kirby's and Bean's persons and the subsequent identification would have been inadmissible as evidence.

"Only after arriving at the police station, and checking the records there, did the arresting officers learn of the Shard robbery. A police car was then dispatched to Shard's place of employment, where it picked up Shard and brought him to the police station. Immediately upon entering the room in the police station where the petitioner and Bean were seated at a table, Shard positively identified them as the men who had robbed him two days earlier. No lawyer was present in the room, and neither the petitioner nor Bean had asked for legal assistance, or been advised of any right to the presence of counsel."[6]

Kirby and Bean were prosecuted for the robbery of Shard. At their trial, Shard testified about the identification at the police station and identified them again in court. The Supreme Court held that the identifications at the station did not violate their constitutional right to the assistance of counsel. Their arrest by itself did not initiate formal criminal proceedings against them, and the Sixth Amendment's guarantee of the right to counsel has historically been applied only after that point.

They were protected, however, by the Due Process Clause of the Fifth and Fourteenth Amendments,* which forbids a lineup that is "unnecessarily suggestive and conducive to irreparable mistaken identification."[7] This standard, unlike the standard of *Wade*, does not automatically exclude an identification made without specific procedural assurances of reliability. Instead, all the circumstances of the identification are considered, and it is excluded only if it fails to meet the minimum requirement of reliability necessary for a fair trial. Among the factors that are considered are "the opportunity of the witness to view the criminal at the time of the crime, the witness' degree of attention, the accuracy of his prior description of the criminal, the level of certainty demonstrated at the confrontation, and the time between the crime and the confrontation."[8] Indications that officers conducting the lineup suggested directly or indirectly whom they expected the witness to identify weigh heavily against reliability.

*See p. 38 above.

Pre-arrest Identification

Sometimes it is necessary to obtain a preliminary identification of a suspect before his arrest, because the identification is necessary to establish probable cause. In such circumstances, the requirement of due process is applicable. Officers may arrange for a witness to observe a suspect on the street, or at his place of work, or in any public place; but they must do so in a way that does not create undue risk of mistaken identification. If possible, the witness should be placed where he can observe a number of people, without being told in advance which of them the police suspect. He might, for example, be asked to look at the people leaving the building where the suspect works at the end of the day. If it is necessary to point out the suspect to the witness, officers should exercise extreme caution not to influence or encourage the witness to make an affirmative identification. The danger of suggestiveness can be reduced by asking the witness to give a description of the criminal before he observes the suspect and, if he makes an identification, to describe in detail the physical features on which he relied.

Photographic Displays

Police often ask an eyewitness to examine photographs of a group of suspects or photographs from a "mug file." This procedure may be essential if a particular suspect has not been identified or there is not probable cause for an arrest and no opportunity can be arranged for the witness to observe a suspect in public. Unlike a lineup, a photographic display can be duplicated afterwards, so that any unfairness in the choice or presentation of photographs can be revealed. Accordingly, the general due process standard of *Kirby* rather than the right to counsel applies to photographic displays conducted *before or after* the beginning of adversary proceedings.[9] To avoid a claim that a display was not fairly conducted and reliable, officers should keep a careful record of the photographs that were used and the manner and order of presentation; the record and the photographs should be preserved for later presentation to the prosecuting authorities and the court.

If a suspect refuses to participate in a lineup, police should not force him to comply. In Chapter 11, we noted generally that officers should not use force to obtain the cooperation of an arrested person at the police station. The use of force at a lineup is particularly to be avoided because it creates the kind of suggestiveness that makes a lineup unreliable. A witness cannot be expected to disregard the fact that one of the persons in the lineup is unwilling to appear. When a person improperly refuses to participate, it may be possible to rely on a photographic display. Or the prosecutor's office may assist the police to obtain a judicial order directing the person to appear in a lineup, failure to comply with which is a contempt of the court. Officers will be able to testify at trial that a person

refused to participate in a lineup; an unexplained refusal is likely to weigh heavily against him.

The constitutional requirements for a valid lineup are not more than safeguards of a reliable identification. As professional officials responsible for criminal investigation, police officers have the strongest reasons of their own to insist on fair and accurate procedures. While taking account of the practical demands of criminal investigation, they should be alert to any risk of mistaken identification and take precautions against it.

Questions for Discussion

1. Describe the conduct of a lineup in your department. What standard procedures are required?

2. On what basis should persons other than the suspect who are to participate in a lineup be chosen? How does your department obtain such persons?

3. Do police have authority to require a person who they believe has committed a crime to participate in a lineup?

4. Does the privilege against compulsory self-incrimination apply to lineup procedures?

5. In what circumstances does the constitutional right to the assistance of counsel apply to lineups? What is the basis for its application to lineups? When it is applicable, what does it require?

6. If the right to the assistance of counsel is not applicable to a lineup or other identification procedure, what constitutional principle does apply?

7. If defense counsel is present when a lineup is conducted, what should he be allowed to do?

8. Describe generally the procedures that should be followed if it is necessary for an eyewitness to view a suspected criminal not in a lineup.

9. What constitutional provision is applicable to photographic displays? Why does the right to counsel not apply to photographic displays after the beginning of formal criminal proceedings?

Problem Cases

There follow the facts of four cases involving eyewitness identifications. In each case, consider carefully the conduct of the identification procedure and decide in light of all the circumstances whether it should have been conducted differently. Then, applying the appropriate constitutional rule, decide whether evidence of the identification should be excluded from the trial.

1. On the day after the armed robbery of a Western Union office, one of the robbers surrendered to the police and implicated Foster ("petitioner") in the robbery.

   "Except for the robbers themselves, the only witness to the crime was Joseph David, the late-night manager of the Western Union office. After Foster had been arrested, David was called to the police station to view a lineup. There were three men in the lineup. One was petitioner. He is a tall man—close to six feet in height. The other two men were short—five feet, five or six inches. Petitioner wore a leather jacket which David said was similar to the one he had seen underneath the coveralls worn by the robber. After seeing this lineup, David could not positively identify petitioner as the robber. He 'thought' he was the man, but he was not sure. David then asked to speak to the petitioner, and petitioner was brought into an office and sat across from David at a table. Except for prosecuting officials there was no one else in the room. Even after this one-to-one confrontation David still was uncertain whether petitioner was one of the robbers: 'truthfully—I was not sure,' he testified at trial. A week or 10 days later, the police arranged for David to view a second lineup. There were five men in that lineup. Petitioner was the only person in the second lineup who had appeared in the first lineup. This time David was 'convinced' petitioner was the man.

   "At trial, David testified to his identification of petitioner in the lineups, as summarized above. He also repeated his identification of petitioner in the courtroom."[10]

2. Biggers ("respondent") was convicted of rape. "...The victim testified at trial that on the evening of January

22...a youth with a butcher knife grabbed her in the doorway to her kitchen:

> 'A.   [H]e grabbed me from behind, and grappled—twisted me on the floor. Threw me down on the floor.
> 'Q.   And there was no light in that kitchen?
> 'A.   Not in the kitchen.
> 'Q.   So you couldn't have seen him then?
> 'A.   Yes, I could see him, when I looked up in his face.
> 'Q.   In the dark?
> 'A.   He was right in the doorway—it was enough light from the bedroom shining through. Yes, I could see who he was.
> 'Q.   You could see? No light? And you could see him and know him then?
> 'A.   Yes.'...

"When the victim screamed, her 12-year-old daughter came out of her bedroom and also began to scream. The assailant directed the victim to 'tell her [the daughter] to shut up, or I'll kill you both.' She did so, and was then walked at knifepoint about two blocks along a railroad track, taken into a woods, and raped there. She testified that 'the moon was shining brightly, full moon.' After the rape, the assailant ran off, and she returned home, the whole incident having taken between 15 minutes and half an hour.

"She then gave the police...[a description of her assailant] describing him as 'being fat and flabby with smooth skin, bushy hair and a youthful voice.' Additionally...[she described him] as being between 16 and 18 years old and between five feet ten inches and six feet tall, as weighing between 180 and 200 pounds, and as having a dark brown complexion....

"On several occasions over the course of the next seven months, she viewed suspects in her home or at the police station, some in lineups and others in showups, and was shown between 30 and 40 photographs. She told the police that the man pictured in one of the photographs had features similar to those of her assailant, but identified none of the suspects. On August 17, the police called her to the station to view respondent, who was being detained on another charge. In an effort to construct a suitable lineup, the police checked the city jail and the city juvenile home. Finding no one at either place fitting respondent's unusual physical description, they conducted a showup instead.

"The showup itself consisted of two detectives walking respondent past the victim. At the victim's request, the police directed respondent to say 'shut up or I'll kill you.' The testimony at trial was not altogether clear as to whether the victim first identified him and then asked that he repeat the words or made her identification after he had spoken. In any event, the victim...had 'no doubt' about her identification....[S]he elaborated in response to questioning.

> 'A.   That I have no doubt, I mean that I am sure that when I—see, when I first laid eyes on him, I knew that it was the individual, because his face—well, there was just something that I don't think I could ever forget. I believe—
>
> 'Q.   You say when you first laid eyes on him, which time are you referring to?
>
> 'A.   When I identified him—when I seen him in the courthouse when I was took up to view the suspect.' "[11]

3.   Brathwaite ("respondent") was convicted of narcotics offenses.

"Jimmy D. Glover, a full-time trooper of the Connecticut State Police...was assigned to the Narcotics Division in an undercover capacity. On May 5...about 7:45 p.m. e.d.t., and while there was still daylight, Glover and Henry Alton Brown, an informant, went to an apartment building at 201 Westland, in Hartford, for the purpose of purchasing narcotics from 'Dickie Boy' Cicero, a known narcotics dealer. Cicero, it was thought, lived on the third floor of that apartment building....Glover and Brown entered the building, observed by backup Officers D'Onofrio and Gaffey, and proceeded by stairs to the third floor. Glover knocked at the door of one of the two apartments served by the stairway. The area was illuminated by natural light from a window in the third floor hallway....The door was opened 12 to 18 inches in response to the knock. Glover observed a man standing at the door and, behind him a woman. Brown identified himself. Glover then asked for 'two things' of narcotics....The man at the door held out his hand, and Glover gave him two $10 bills. The door closed. Soon the man returned and handed Glover two glassine bags. While the door was open, Glover stood within two feet of the person from whom he made the purchase and observed his face. Five to seven minutes elapsed from the time the door first opened until it closed the second time....

"Glover and Brown then left the building. This was about eight minutes after their arrival. Glover drove to headquarters where he described the seller to D'Onofrio and Gaffey. Glover at that time did not know the identity of the seller....He described him as being 'a colored man, approximately five feet eleven inches tall, dark complexion, black hair, short Afro style, and having high cheekbones, and of heavy build. He was wearing at the time blue pants and a plaid shirt.'...D'Onofrio, suspecting from this description that respondent might be the seller, obtained a photograph of respondent from the Records Division of the Hartford Police Department. He left it at Glover's office. D'Onofrio was not acquainted with respondent personally, but did know him by sight and had seen him '[s]everal times' prior to May 5.... Glover, when alone, viewed the photograph for the first time upon his return to headquarters on May 7; he identified the person shown as the one from whom he had purchased the narcotics....

"The toxicological report on the contents of the glassine bags revealed the presence of heroin. The report was dated July 16....

"Respondent was arrested on July 27 while visiting at the apartment of a Mrs. Ramsey on the third floor of 201 Westland. This was the apartment at which the narcotics sale had taken place on May 5.

"Respondent was charged, in a two-count information, with possession and sale of heroin.... At his trial in January...the photograph from which Glover had identified respondent was received in evidence without objection on the part of the defense.... Glover also testified that, although he had not seen respondent in the eight months that had elapsed since the sale, 'there [was] no doubt whatsoever' in his mind that the person shown on the photograph was respondent....Glover also made a positive in-court identification without objection....

"No explanation was offered by the prosecution for the failure to utilize a photographic array or to conduct a lineup."[12]

4. Stovall ("petitioner") was convicted of murder.

"Dr. Paul Behrendt was stabbed to death in the kitchen of his home in Garden City, Long Island, about midnight August 23.... Dr. Behrendt's wife, also a physician, had followed her husband to the kitchen and jumped at the assailant. He knocked her to the floor and stabbed her 11 times. The police found a shirt on the kitchen floor and keys in a pocket which they traced to petitioner. They arrested him on the afternoon of August 24. An arraignment was promptly held but was postponed until petitioner could retain counsel.

"Mrs. Behrendt was hospitalized for major surgery to save her life. The police, without affording petitioner time to retain counsel, arranged with her surgeon to permit them to bring petitioner to her hospital room about noon of August 25, the day after the surgery. Petitioner was handcuffed to one of five police officers who, with two members of the staff of the District Attorney, brought him to the hospital room. Petitioner was the only Negro in the room. Mrs. Behrendt identified him from her hospital bed after being asked by an officer whether he 'was the man' and after petitioner repeated at the direction of an officer 'a few words for voice identification.' None of the witnesses could recall the words that were used. Mrs. Behrendt and the officers testified at the trial to her identification of the petitioner in the hospital room, and she also made an in-court identification of petitioner in the courtroom."[13]

Notes

1. Kirby v. Illinois, 406 U.S. 682, 689 (1972).
2. United States v. Wade, 388 U.S. 218, 220 (1967).
3. *Id.* at 228 (footnote omitted).
4. *Id.* at 239.
5. *Id.* at 240.
6. Kirby v. Illinois, 406 U.S. 682, 684–85 (1972) (footnote omitted).

7. *Id.* at 691.

8. Manson v. Brathwaite, 432 U.S. 98, 114 (1977).

9. United States v. Ash, 413 U.S. 300 (1973). See generally Simmons v. United States, 390 U.S. 377 (1968).

10. Foster v. California, 394 U.S. 440, 441–42 (1969).

11. Neil v. Biggers, 409 U.S. 188, 193–96 (1972)(footnote omitted).

12. Manson v. Brathwaite, 432 U.S. 98, 99–102 (1977) (footnotes omitted).

13. Stovall v. Denno, 388 U.S. 293, 295 (1967).

CHAPTER 13

QUESTIONING

The questioning of suspects is one of those topics in the law of criminal investigation that always provoke controversy, as if there were no middle ground. To those who favor such questioning, it is simply part of an investigation. Once police have arrested someone whom they have probable cause to believe is guilty, it is reasonable and proper to ask him about the crime and try to obtain evidence about it. So long as he is not abused, there is no objection to persistent, even intensive, questioning. To those who oppose such questioning, it smacks of oppression. Someone who has been arrested should not be encouraged to give evidence against his own interest. The government should get its evidence of guilt elsewhere.

If a person has confessed that he committed a crime and continues to admit his guilt, there is ordinarily no problem about the earlier confession. A problem arises when a defendant who has confessed or made a damaging admission later denies his guilt and requires the government to prove its case. Then the prosecutor may want to use the prior confession or admission as evidence of guilt at the trial. That can be done by calling as a witness an officer who heard the defendant's statement or by offering in evidence a statement written or subscribed by him. The defendant may then oppose the admission of this evidence on the ground that the confession was obtained in violation of his constitutional rights.

Constitutional law on this subject has undergone considerable development and change, including some shifts in the particular provision of the Constitution on which the courts have relied. Throughout this development, however, a small number of issues and principles have remained of central importance. Recently the well-known *Miranda* rules have focused attention still more narrowly. We shall consider first the development of the constitutional law and the basic principles and then examine in detail the *Miranda* rules and their application. Separate principles based on the constitutional right to the assistance of counsel restrict efforts to elicit information from a person once he has been formally accused of a crime. Another section of this chapter discusses those restrictions.

Voluntary Confessions

It is a settled principle of constitutional law that only a voluntary confession, one that is the product of the defendant's free and unconstrained choice, can be used in evidence against him. In the decade before World War II, the Supreme Court decided several cases in which a defendant was convicted of a crime partly on the basis of a confession extracted by torture. In one such case, three defendants were arrested on a charge of murder. One of them was hung on a tree and whipped repeatedly until he confessed to all the details of the crime. The other two were likewise whipped until they confessed. They were told that if they changed their story at any time, the torture would be renewed. On the following day, they repeated their confessions before witnesses, whose testimony about the confessions was the basis of the defendants' convictions at trial. The Supreme Court reversed the convictions. It said: "It would be difficult to conceive of methods more revolting to the sense of justice than those taken to procure the confessions...."[1]

There is no need for discussion about such a case. Even if one believed that the defendants were guilty of the murder—and, of course, confessions obtained by such methods are worthless as evidence of guilt—no civilized community can regard torture by public officials as legitimate criminal investigation. While other cases involving actual or threatened physical torture have occasionally arisen, everyone agrees that such practices do not reflect the standards of the police as a profession any more than those of the society generally.

Most confession cases have not involved a claim of physical abuse. The claim that the courts have usually been asked to consider is that the defendant's confession was involuntary because it was given after the police had questioned him intensively, in circumstances that deprived him of freedom of choice. In such cases, the courts have been required not only to determine the precise facts surrounding the confession, which are often in dispute, but also to declare what is meant by a voluntary confession and what kinds of facts make a confession involuntary.

Spano v. New York

Spano was indicted for first-degree murder. He was alleged to have shot a man after a fight in a bar. A warrant was issued for his arrest. While he was still at large, he called a close friend named Bruno, who had recently joined the police force. He told Bruno that he intended to hire a lawyer and surrender to the police.

"The following day, February 4, at 7:10 p.m., petitioner [Spano], accompanied by counsel, surrendered himself to the authorities in front of the Bronx County Building, where both the office of the Assistant District Attorney who ultimately prosecuted his case and the courtroom in which he was ultimately tried were located. His attorney had cautioned him to answer no questions, and left him in the custody of the officers. He was promptly taken to the office of the Assistant District Attorney and at 7:15 p.m. the questioning began, being conducted by Assistant District Attorney Goldsmith, Lt. Gannon, Detectives Farrell, Lehrer and Motta, and Sgt. Clarke. The record reveals that the questioning was both persistent and continuous. Petitioner, in accordance with his attorney's instructions, steadfastly refused to answer. Detective Motta testified: 'He refused to talk to me.' 'He just looked up to the ceiling and refused to talk to me.' Detective Farrell testified:

'Q. And you started to interrogate him?
'A. That is right.
'Q. What did he say?

'A. He said 'you would have to see my attorney. I tell you nothing but my name.'
'Q. Did you continue to examine him?
'A. Verbally, yes, sir.'

He asked one officer, Detective Ciccone, if he could speak to his attorney, but that request was denied. Detective Ciccone testified that he could not find the attorney's name in the telephone book. He was given two sandwiches, coffee and cake at 11 p.m.

"At 12:15 a.m. on the morning of February 5, after five hours of questioning in which it became evident that petitioner was following his attorney's instructions, on the Assistant District Attorney's orders petitioner was transferred to the 46th Squad, Ryer Avenue Police Station. The Assistant District Attorney also went to the police station and to some extent continued to participate in the interrogation. Petitioner arrived at 12:30 and questioning was resumed at 12:40. The character of the questioning is revealed by the testimony of Detective Farrell:

'Q. Who did you leave him in the room with?
'A. With Detective Lehrer and Sergeant Clarke came in and Mr. Goldsmith came in or Inspector Halk came in. It was back and forth. People just came in, spoke a few words to the defendant or they listened a few minutes and they left.

But petitioner persisted in his refusal to answer, and again requested permission to see his attorney, this time from Detective Lehrer. His request was again denied.

"It was then that those in charge of the investigation decided that petitioner's close friend, Bruno, could be of use. He had been called out on the case around 10 or 11 p.m., although he was not connected with the 46th Squad or Precinct in any way. Although, in fact, his job was in no way threatened, Bruno was told to tell petitioner that petitioner's telephone call had gotten him 'in a lot of trouble,' and that he should seek to extract sympathy from petitioner for Bruno's pregnant wife and three children. Bruno developed this theme with petitioner without success, and petitioner, also without success, again sought to see his attorney, a request which Bruno relayed unavailingly to his superiors. After this first session with petitioner, Bruno was again directed by Lt. Gannon to play on petitioner's sympathies, but again no confession was forthcoming. But the Lieutenant a third time ordered Bruno falsely to importune his friend to confess, but again petitioner clung to his attorney's advice. Inevitably, in the fourth such session directed by the Lieutenant, lasting a full hour, petitioner succumbed to his friend's prevarications and agreed to make a statement. Accordingly, at 3:25 a.m. the Assistant District Attorney, a stenographer, and several other law enforcement officials entered the room where petitioner was being questioned, and took his statement in question and answer form with the Assistant District Attorney asking the questions. The statement was completed at 4:05 a.m.

"But this was not the end. At 4:30 a.m. three detectives took petitioner to Police Headquarters in Manhattan. On the way they attempted to find the bridge from which petitioner said he had thrown the murder weapon. They crossed the Triborough Bridge into Manhattan, arriving at Police Headquarters at 5 a.m., and left Manhattan for the Bronx at 5:40 a.m. via the Willis Avenue Bridge. When petitioner recognized neither bridge as the one from which he had thrown the weapon, they reentered Manhattan via the Third Avenue Bridge, which petitioner stated was the right one, and then returned to the Bronx well after 6 a.m. During that trip the officers also elicited a statement from petitioner that the deceased was always 'on [his] back,' 'always pushing' him and that he was 'not sorry' he had shot the deceased. All three detectives testified to that statement at the trial.

"Court opened at 10 a.m. that morning, and petitioner was arraigned at 10:15.

. . .

"Petitioner was a foreign-born young man of 25 with no past history of law violation or of subjection to official interrogation, at least insofar as the record shows. He had progressed only one-half year into high school and the record indicates that he had a history of emotional instability. He did not make a narrative statement, but was subject to the leading questions of a skillful prosecutor in a question and answer confession. He was subjected to questioning not by a few men, but by many. They included Assistant District Attorney Goldsmith, one Hyland of the District Attorney's Office, Deputy Inspector Halks, Lieutenant Gannon, Detective Ciccone, Detective Motta, Detective Lehrer, Detective Marshal, Detective Farrell, Detective Leira, Detective Murphy, Detective Murtha, Sergeant Clarke, Patrolman Bruno and Stenographer Baldwin. All played some part, and the effect of such massive official interrogation must have been felt.

Petitioner was questioned for virtually eight straight hours before he confessed, with his only respite being a transfer to an arena presumably considered more appropriate by the police for the task at hand. Nor was the questioning conducted during normal business hours, but began in early evening, continued into the night, and did not bear fruition until the not-too-early morning. The drama was not played out, with the final admissions obtained, until almost sunrise. In such circumstances slowly mounting fatigue does, and is calculated to, play its part. The questioners persisted in the face of his repeated refusals to answer on the advice of his attorney and they ignored his reasonable requests to contact the local attorney whom he had already retained and who had personally delivered him into the custody of these officers in obedience to the bench warrant.

"The use of Bruno, characterized in this Court by counsel for the State as a 'childhood friend' of petitioner's, is another factor which deserves mention in the totality of the situation. Bruno's was the one face visible to petitioner in which he could put some trust. There was a bond of friendship between them going back a decade into adolescence. It was with this material that the officers felt that they could overcome petitioner's will. They instructed Bruno falsely to state that Petitioner's telephone call had gotten him into trouble, that his job was in jeopardy, and that loss of his job would be disastrous to his three children, his wife and his unborn child. And Bruno played this part of a worried father, harried by his superiors, in not one, but four different acts, the final one lasting an hour...."[2]

The Supreme Court held that Spano's confession was not voluntary and should not have been admitted at his trial, because his "will was overborne by official pressure, fatigue and sympathy falsely aroused."[3]

Other cases in which the voluntariness of a confession was at issue present distinct facts. As in *Spano*, all the circumstances of the confession have to be considered. The pattern when a confession is found to have been involuntary is the defendant's initial refusal to give information about the crime, followed by officers' persistent, intensive questioning, confrontations with witnesses or accusers, and the like, all manifesting the officers' fixed purpose to overcome the defendant's unwillingness to speak. When all the facts—the duration of the questioning, typically incommunicado detention, more or less explicit intimidation or humiliation of the defendant—are considered together, they indicate more than questioning in hope of an answer; they indicate an effort to obtain answers *despite* the defendant's intention not to confess. Since the critical issue of voluntariness refers to the defendant's state of mind when the confession is given rather than to the methods of the officers as such, the personal characteristics of the defendant are relevant. A defendant who is young, or unsophisticated, or emotionally unstable (like Spano) may yield to pressure more easily than a street-wise adult who has had prior experience with the police.

The constitutional basis for the principle that an involuntary confession is not admissible is the Due Process Clause.* The privilege against compulsory self-incrimination, which we shall examine below, and a well-established rule of evidence against the use of involuntary confessions also support the principle. All of these sources contribute to its rationale. It is clear that any method to obtain a confession that would make it unreliable is impermissible. Society's interest in investigating crime and prosecuting criminals is not served by the conviction of a person whom the evidence does not show reliably to be guilty. Accordingly, the Constitution prohibits the use of a confession obtained by questioning so prolonged, intensive, or suggestive that one has doubt whether the person questioned knew or cared about what he was saying.

In addition, a confession must be the defendant's own act. The government is not obliged to rely on a confession; it may, if it can, prove the defendant's guilt entirely by other evidence. If the government does rely on the defendant's confession, it must at the same time respect his independent capacity as a human being and not treat him simply as a potential source of evidence. It is worth recalling that when police question a suspect, he

---

*See p. 38 above.

has not been proved guilty. Belief, even strong belief, that he has committed a crime gives no basis for public officials to disregard the ordinary respect that the government owes an individual in our society.

The Privilege Against Compulsory Self-Incrimination

The Fifth Amendment provides that no person "shall be compelled in any criminal case to be a witness against himself." Although the requirement that a confession be voluntary is based on the Due Process Clause, it is also closely related to this provision of the Fifth Amendment. In ordinary language, we would say that if someone has been *compelled* to do something, he has not done it *voluntarily*. In the famous *Miranda* case,[4] the Supreme Court shifted the focus in confession cases from the Due Process Clause to the privilege against compulsory self-incrimination. In order to protect the privilege, the Court announced a set of rules that officers are required to follow when they question a person who is in custody. Failure to follow the rules has the effect that any confession or admission that the person makes during the questioning cannot be used against him.

A major reason for this change was the difficulty of deciding in a close case whether a confession was voluntary. Too often, the result depended on a doubtful judgment about that issue, with which many people disagreed. Also, the Supreme Court expressed its concern that unless standard procedures were developed for all custodial interrogation, there could be no assurance that the "third degree" was entirely eliminated. The Court was concerned particularly about the use of psychological techniques for inducing a person to confess. Manuals about how to question a suspect recommend such practices as isolating the person, expressing false sympathy or certainty that he is guilty, alternating kindness and hostility, and a variety of deliberate deceptions and trickery. The plain purpose of these practices, the Court said, is to make the person questioned submit to the will of the questioner. Far from taking steps to ensure that a decision to confess is freely made, the questioner tries to achieve his purpose without regard to the person's independent choice. And even if psychological tactics are not used, questioning a suspect while he is detained at the police station exerts pressure to respond that is inconsistent with the privilege against compulsory self-incrimination.

The Court's conclusion was that unless affirmative steps are taken to eliminate the pressure of questioning at the police station, there can be no assurance that a confession was not obtained in violation of the constitutional privilege. It did not say that every confession obtained during police interrogation was in fact compelled, but that without safeguards against compulsion we cannot be sure that it was not compelled. Therefore, only if the *Miranda* rules are followed can a confession be used. On the other hand, if the rules are followed, that ordinarily satisfies the requirement of voluntariness without further inquiry. Police are sometimes troubled by the apparent rigidity of the *Miranda* rules. It is worthwhile to recall that part of their purpose is to do away with the uncertainties of the earlier standard.

The Miranda Rules

The *Miranda* rules were prescribed by the Supreme Court to eliminate the compelling pressures of *custodial interrogation,* which it defined as "questioning initiated by law enforcement officers after a person has been taken into custody or otherwise deprived of his freedom of action in any significant way."[5] The rules, briefly stated, require that before any questioning the person be warned:

1. *that he has the right to remain silent,*

2. *that anything he says may be used as evidence against him, and*

3. *that he has the right to have an attorney present while he is questioned.*

If he indicates at any time that he does not want to be questioned or that he wants to talk to a lawyer, questioning must stop.

If a person has been given the necessary warnings and is willing to be questioned, officers can question him. But the warnings cannot be omitted for any reason. Failure to give the warning is not excused even by proof that the person already knew his rights. Interpretation of the rules in particular circumstances is discussed in more detail below. If their purpose, to ensure that a person's statements in response to questioning are given freely, is kept in mind and fully honored, officers will seldom have difficulty in applying them.

Custodial Interrogation

The Supreme Court's reasoning in *Miranda* depended a good deal on the pressure to confess likely to be felt by someone who is questioned at a police station. Although such interrogation was what the Court had most in mind, the *Miranda* rules are not limited to the station. They apply to any questioning initiated by the police after a person is in custody and is no longer free to go. Soon after the *Miranda* case was decided, one police department is said to have transported arrested persons to the station by the longer "scenic route," on the theory that the rules might not apply to questioning in the police car. Everyone must recognize that constitutional requirements are not so easily evaded, simply by changing the place where the questioning occurs.

Deliberate questioning should be distinguished from a situation in which an officer's actions while making an arrest or performing ordinary peace-keeping duties elicits a response. Suppose an officer comes to the scene of a disturbance on the street, stops several persons who appear to be involved and says, "What's going on?" If one of the persons answers the question and incriminates himself, have the *Miranda* rules been violated because he was stopped and was not given the necessary warning before the question was asked? Surely not. An officer performing his peace-keeping function is not required to act in strict silence. But once the officer's purpose changes to an effort to obtain information about a crime from someone who is then in custody, the *Miranda* rules apply.

Orozco v. Texas

"The evidence introduced at trial showed that petitioner [Orozco] and the deceased had quarreled outside the El Farleto Cafe in Dallas shortly before midnight on the date of the shooting. The deceased had apparently spoken to petitioner's female companion inside the restaurant. In the heat of the quarrel outside, the deceased is said to have beaten petitioner about the face and called him 'Mexican Grease.' A shot was fired killing the deceased. Petitioner left the scene and returned to his boardinghouse to sleep. At about 4 a.m. four police officers arrived at petitioner's boardinghouse, were admitted by an unidentified woman, and were told that petitioner was asleep in the bedroom. All four officers entered the bedroom and began to question petitioner. From the moment he gave his name, according to the testimony of one of the officers, petitioner was not free to go where he pleased but was 'under arrest.' The officers asked him if he had been to the El Farleto restaurant that night and when he answered 'yes' he was asked if he owned a pistol. Petitioner admitted owning one. After being asked a second time where the pistol was located, he admitted that it was in the washing machine in a backroom of the boardinghouse. Ballistics tests indicated that the gun found in the washing machine was the gun that fired the fatal shot."[6]

At trial, one of the arresting officers testified about Orozco's responses to the questions asked in his bedroom. The Supreme Court concluded that the testimony should not have been admitted, because the questions were asked without compliance with the *Miranda* rules.

The *Orozco* case indicates how far the concept of custodial interrogation is extended and how alert to the need for *Miranda* warnings an arresting officer has to be. One might reasonably argue that the few questions that Orozco was asked in the course of the arrest did not constitute the pressured questioning against which the rules guard. The surest course for an officer is to assume that the *Miranda* rules apply and give the warnings as soon as he deliberately questions any person whom he has arrested or who may reasonably believe that he is no longer free to go. Such a practice consistently followed will allow a line to be drawn between a police operation not intended specifically to elicit information and deliberate questioning.

Some efforts have been made to extend the concept of custodial interrogation to situations in which a person is the target of an investigation but has not been arrested. In one case, an officer asked a parolee to come to the police station, where the officer questioned him about a burglary. Before the questioning began, the officer told the parolee that he was not under arrest; after the questioning, he was allowed to leave although he had admitted his guilt. The Supreme Court concluded that since he was not actually in custody, the questioning was not custodial interrogation.[7] The *Miranda* rules apply only if there has been an actual interruption of the person's liberty. However, if a person reasonably believes that he is not free to go, an officer's undisclosed intention not to make an arrest does not make *Miranda* inapplicable. If there may be doubt, a cautious officer will either advise a person whom he is about to question that he is not in custody and is not required to remain, or give the *Miranda* warnings.

Even if a person has been arrested and is clearly in custody, *Miranda* warnings are not required unless he is questioned. A person who volunteers incriminating statements to an officer without having been questioned cannot later complain that he was not given the warnings. On the other hand, "interrogation" is not limited to explicit questioning, when an officer asks questions and expects or hopes for an answer. It includes any conduct of officers likely to have the same effect. "...[T]he term 'interrogation' under *Miranda* refers not only to express questioning, but also to any words or actions on the part of the police (other than those normally attendant to arrest and custody) that the police should know are reasonably likely to elicit an incriminating response from the suspect."[8]

An officer who is accompanying an arrested person to the stationhouse should not engage in a discussion about the crime even if no questions are asked, unless *Miranda* warnings have been given. Similarly, two or more officers in the company of someone whom they have arrested should not discuss the crime in terms likely to elicit a response from him, unless the warnings have been given. Officers should be particularly careful not to make statements to the person or to one another that are calculated to excite remorse or worry or anger, which may in turn prompt incriminating remarks.

It may seem an unreasonable and artificial extension of the privilege against compulsory self-incrimination to prohibit officers from talking to a person whom they have arrested or talking in his presence about the crime. The rules that we have been considering do not go that far. Officers are not required to keep silent. But if their speech and conduct are likely to have the same effect on the person as would deliberate questioning, they are required to give the *Miranda* warnings to ensure that he does not unwillingly submit to the pressure of custodial interrogation in any form. Rather than assume that no warnings need be given unless and until explicit questioning is about to begin, an officer who has made an arrest and will be together with the person for some time before he arrives at the station should give the warnings promptly. Then, if the person makes an incriminating statement later, there will not be doubt about its admissibility in evidence.

The Conduct of Questioning

Once the necessary warnings have been given, police may question a person in custody only if he is willing to be questioned; he has a right not to answer or to be questioned at all. If he is willing to be questioned only on certain conditions, the officer must choose whether to meet the conditions or not to question. Most important, if he agrees to be questioned only after he has spoken with his lawyer or only in his lawyer's presence, that condition must be met. Once a person has indicated that he wishes to consult with his lawyer, all questioning must stop; and officers may not initiate questioning later in the absence of a lawyer, even if they repeat the *Miranda* warnings a second time and obtain the person's consent to be questioned.[9] Furthermore, he may change his mind at any time. If, having initially agreed, he refuses to be questioned further, his refusal must be accepted.

No particular expression of consent to be questioned is required. However, an officer who questions without having obtained an explicit expression of consent orally or in writing, will have difficulty convincing a court that the person really was willing to be questioned; the Supreme Court has said that in such a case, the prosecution has a heavy burden of proof.[10] An officer who is eager to question someone may find it easy to believe that the person is willing to be questioned, even though his expression of willingness is ambiguous. In the *Miranda* opinion, the Supreme Court indicated that doubts of this kind should be resolved against questioning. An officer may try to resolve a doubt, provided that he does not exert the coercive pressure that the *Miranda* rules are intended to avoid.

If doubt remains, little can be accomplished by ignoring it and proceeding to question. The result will at best be a contest at trial about the admissibility of incriminating statements that are obtained. If it is found that the questioning was not proper, later statements of the person may also be excluded as "fruits" of the original illegality. It is a far wiser course and more consistent with the spirit of the *Miranda* decision not to question in such circumstances. If the person subsequently indicates that he is willing to be questioned, there will be no problem about his having been questioned prematurely.

A consistent practice of giving the *Miranda* requirements full and conscientious effect will help to resolve questions that may arise in particular circumstances. An officer should keep in mind the constitutional purpose of the *Miranda* rules and use his common sense accordingly. He should ask himself whether an observer who is especially concerned to protect the arrested person's right not to be compelled to speak would consider that the circumstances manifest the kind of pressure that renders questioning improper or, on the other hand, manifest the person's willingness to be questioned. It is well to recall also that if a person is willing to be questioned, it will do no harm to make his willingness fully clear. If his willingness is doubtful, then *Miranda* requires that the doubt be removed before questioning takes place.

Unsurprisingly, the *Miranda* rules have been the subject of much debate and have frequently been criticized. As the Supreme Court acknowledged, the rules were intended to guard against the *danger* of compulsion or intimidation during questioning; therefore, they may appear to impose rigid requirements even in circumstances when questioning without them would not depart from constitutional standards. Police have little to regret about *Miranda*. The rules have not hampered officers in their conduct of criminal investigation. Conscientious adherence is not difficult and consumes little time. It gives reassurance both at the time of questioning and in subsequent legal proceedings that the Constitution has been respected. In a difficult or ambiguous situation, an officer can rely on the *Miranda* rules rather than having to determine for himself how to proceed. It is easy to suppose that any protection afforded criminals against incriminating themselves must be a new obstacle for the police. *Miranda* can as easily be regarded as a simplification of their work and an aid in its performance.*

The Right to Counsel

In Chapter 12, we considered the Sixth Amendment's guarantee of the right to counsel and noted that it applies only to lineups conducted after the start of formal criminal proceedings. Similarly, once proceedings have begun—when a person has been formally accused by indictment or information, or has been brought before a magistrate for a hearing at which he is advised of the charges against him—the right to counsel prohibits investigating officers from questioning the defendant or making any equivalent effort to obtain information about the

---

*In the original *Miranda* opinion, the Supreme Court suggested that all use of a statement obtained in violation of the rules was prohibited. More recently, the Court has allowed the use of such statements in some circumstances, notably when the defendant makes a contradictory statement at trial. While those cases are of importance to prosecutors and defense counsel, they are not of special significance for police, whose responsibility is to comply with *Miranda*. The fact that a statement obtained in violation of *Miranda* may later be admitted at trial does not lessen the violation itself.

crime from him, unless he has the assistance of his lawyer or has waived his right to such assistance.

The application of this constitutional rule is unlike the *Miranda* requirements, which are not limited to the stage of adversary proceedings. Once the right to counsel applies, *any* effort by police to obtain information directly from the defendant in the absence of counsel is prohibited, whether or not there is custodial interrogation and whether or not the *Miranda* warnings are given. Three cases illustrate the broad scope of this rule.

Massiah v. United States

Massiah had been indicted for narcotics offenses. While he was released on bail, a confederate in the offenses decided to cooperate with the investigators. He arranged to have a conversation with Massiah in the former's car. An investigator overheard Massiah's incriminating statements by means of a transmitter concealed in the car.[11]

The Supreme Court held that the secret transmission of the conversation was the equivalent of questioning without the assistance of counsel and that Massiah's statements could not be used against him.

Brewer v. Williams

Williams, who had recently escaped from a mental hospital, was arrested in Davenport, Iowa, for the abduction of a young girl in Des Moines, 160 miles away. He was given *Miranda* warnings. While Des Moines detectives were coming to Davenport to pick him up, Williams was brought before a magistrate, who advised him of his rights and committed him to jail. Williams also spoke with a lawyer, who advised him to make no statements to the police. During the ride back to Des Moines, one of the two detectives talked about the difficulty of locating the abducted girl's body and the importance of giving her a burial before snow fell. Before the trip ended, Williams made incriminating statements and finally led the detectives to the girl's body.[12]

Concluding that the detective's purpose in talking to Williams in the car was to elicit incriminating statements and that the conversation was the equivalent of questioning, the Supreme Court held that Williams' statements were obtained in violation of his right to the assistance of counsel. (Notice that this ruling is not affected by the fact that Williams was given *Miranda* warnings.)

United States v. Henry

Henry had been indicted for bank robbery and was detained in jail and awaiting trial. A government agent investigating the robbery contacted an inmate at the jail who worked as a paid informant for the FBI. The inmate told the agent that he was housed in the cellblock with Henry and other federal prisoners. The agent asked him to be alert to any incriminating statements that the federal prisoners made but not to question Henry or initiate any conversations with him about the robbery. Henry talked to the inmate about the robbery and the conversations were reported to the agent.[13]

The Supreme Court concluded that Henry's incriminating statements were obtained in violation of his right to the assistance of counsel, because they had been deliberately elicted by someone acting in the capacity of an agent for the government.*

The critical factor in each of these cases is that official action was deliberately undertaken to obtain

---

*On the informer's status as a government agent, see pp. 128–129 above.

incriminating statements. The right to the assistance of counsel does not prevent police from receiving information about a crime after criminal proceedings have begun. If a private person volunteers information about the defendant, it is proper for the police to use the information, as they use any evidence that is uncovered in late stages of an investigation. But the police may not themselves or through an intermediary purposely arrange a situation in which the defendant is likely to make incriminating statements.

The police effort to elicit incriminating statements in *Massiah* and *Williams* is evident. In *Henry*, it is less clear. One might argue reasonably that the informer inmate was only a passive recipient of information volunteered by Henry. The ruling of the Supreme Court indicates that once criminal proceedings have begun, almost any effort by an officer to obtain statements from the defendant without full disclosure and opportunity for him to be advised by counsel will violate his right under the Sixth Amendment. When a potential informer, like the inmate in *Henry*, offers to obtain information from someone against whom proceedings have begun, the officer should be careful not to say or do anything that establishes a working relationship and makes the informer an agent of the police. If that is avoided, information that he obtains will be admissible in evidence.

Further Applications of the Privilege Against Compulsory Self-Incrimination

The privilege against compulsory self-incrimination provides a general formula defining the government's authority to obtain information from someone about crimes he may have committed. Many of its applications are not concerned with questioning by the police or with the work of the police at all. Issues involving the privilege arise at various stages of the prosecution, after investigation of the crime has been completed.

One aspect of the privilege that we have not considered elsewhere may have importance for the police. Occasionally, officers have reason to search for and seize documents prepared by a person who is himself incriminated by them. Officers investigating fraudulent transactions, for example, may have probable cause to search for and seize records of the transactions prepared by the person who they believe is guilty of fraud. The Fourth Amendment's requirements must, of course, be observed in any such search. The privilege against compulsory self-incrimination, however, has no appliction, even though the documents incriminate the person who prepared them. The privilege applies only if the government compels the act that incriminates. Since the records were prepared without any compulsion and their seizure requires no incriminating act by the suspect, there is no compulsory self-incrimination.[14] This may not be true if the papers are sought by a subpoena or court order directed to a person whom the papers incriminate. Then, the person's act of producing the papers may incriminate him because he tacitly affirms that the papers produced are the ones named in the subpoena; and if so, the privilege is applicable because the subpoena constitutes compulsion.[15] Before seeking to obtain documents by a court order, officers should consult with the prosecutor's office, as one would expect them to do ordinarily before appearing in court.

A few other general principles explain applications of the privilege against compulsory self-incrimination outside the context of police work. 'Incrimination'' does not mean merely giving information about a crime that one has committed. Rather, it means giving information that may subject oneself to prosecution. Therefore, if a person has already been prosecuted and cannot be prosecuted again or if he has some other protection against prosecution, like a statute of limitations, he can be required to testify about his criminal conduct before a grand jury or otherwise by a court order. That rule has led to the enactment of immunity statutes, which enable a prosecuting official, through the court, to give a person immunity from prosecution on the basis of his testimony and then to require him to respond to questions. Immunity does not protect the person from prosecution for the crime altogether; it provides only that his testimony cannot be used in any way to further his prosecution.

The compulsion prohibited by the privilege is not limited to force, threats, or explicit penalties for failure to give information. Any official harm that follows from a refusal to give self-incriminating information is prohibited. In one case the Supreme Court held that police officers who were being investigated for "fixing" traffic tickets could not be compelled to incriminate themselves by the threat of being fired if they asserted the constitutional privilege.[16] However, public officials (including police officers) who refuse to give information when it is required as a part of their duties can be fired for failure to perform their duties properly; the fact that the information might be incriminating does not relieve them of their ordinary responsibility.[17] Finally, it should be noted that the privilege protects againt incrimination of oneself only. It affords no protection against compulsion to testify against anyone else, including friends and members of one's family.

Questions for Discussion

1. What provision of the Constitution is the basis for the requirement that a confession be voluntary?

2. What is meant by a voluntary confession?
   What test is applied to determine whether a confession is voluntary?

3. What are the *Miranda* rules?

4. What provision of the Constitution is the source of the *Miranda* rules?

5. Explain the reasoning that led the Supreme Court to adopt the *Miranda* rules.

6. In what circumstances is it necessary to give the *Miranda* warnings?

7. What is meant by custodial interrogation?

8. How does the start of formal criminal proceedings affect the authority of police to seek evidence directly from the accused person?
   Why does it have this effect?

Problem Cases

In each of the following cases, consider what constitutional objections might be made to the conduct of the police officer(s). How should a court respond to the objections? Consider also how you might have conducted the investigation differently, to avoid constitutional objections.

1. Having reason to believe that Hall was implicated in a bank robbery that had occurred earlier in the day but lacking probable cause for his arrest, three federal agents went to his home, a small apartment "with a living room some 12' × 14' furnished with a couch and two chairs, a kitchen, a bedroom and bath." They identified themselves and asked to speak with him about the bank robbery and explained why they were interested in him. After Hall had answered questions for seventeen minutes, the agents asked for permission to make a search, which he gave. Nothing was found in the search. The agents then gave the defendant the *Miranda* warnings and the questioning resumed. During the first seventeen minutes, Hall made statements that were incriminating.[18]

2. Suspecting that Duffy had been involved in a robbery in which one of the victims had been stabbed, Officer Nevin went to the home of Duffy's girlfriend where Duffy was staying. He was admitted and taken to a bedroom where Duffy was asleep. "...[U]pon entering the room...[Nevin] noticed a knife sticking out from under the mattress of Duffy's bed and, before arousing the latter, he withdrew it. He then woke Duffy and greeted him with the query, 'is this the knife you used in the fight?' ...Duffy's response was, 'no, I had it with me and I dropped it during the fight. Joe Louis picked it up. Then I got it back. I don't know who stabbed the guy." Nevin then placed Duffy under arrest.[19]

3. Shortly after a fatal stabbing on a public street, "as a result of a phone call from headquarters, Police Officer Edward Hollingsworth, who was on patrol, proceeded to the hospital to investigate. In the hospital accident ward, he found several persons, including...Jefferson, who had a towel over her forehead and left eye....

"Upon entering the hospital accident ward, Hollingsworth asked: 'What happened?' Jefferson replied: 'There was a fight.'... 'They jumped me and I stabbed them.'"[20]

4. Officers arrested Daniel W. for car theft. W. told them that Rodney P. was his accomplice. P. was sixteen years old. The officers went to P.'s home at about 8:00 p.m. and found him standing with two friends by the side of the house. An officer asked the two friends to leave and then questioned P. for about four minutes. P. admitted that he had taken the car. The officer then took P. inside the house and spoke to his father about his arrest.[21]

5. "At approximately 9:15 p.m. . . . nine Houston police officers, carrying a valid search warrant and firearms, entered a downtown drugstore of which Kenneth Jordan Brown was the manager. The warrant authorized a search for narcotics, and the affidavit upon which it was issued named Brown as the possessor of the suspected contraband. The doors of the store were closed, and Brown was summoned from a back room, where he had been lying down, to witness the officers as they searched the premises. After the store had been carefully searched for a period of 30 to 45 minutes, one of the officers discovered a brown paper sack under a display counter which contained two plastic bags filled with a substance later determined to be heroin. As the officer raised the sack from its place of concealment, he exhibited it to Brown and asked him 'What is this?' Brown replied: 'It's heroin. You've got me this time.' "[22]

6. "Catanzaro was indicted with three others for the holdup killing of a United Parcel truckdriver on May 17 . . . on 53rd Street near Second Avenue in New York City. As a result of thorough police investigation . . . [he] was discovered to be staying in a certain hotel and detectives went there to apprehend him. . . . [Catanzaro] having gone out, the detectives awaited his return; two of them were let into the room by the hotel clerk, while a third remained in the lobby. . . . [Catanzaro] arrived at about one o'clock in the morning, carrying a package under his left arm. Spotted by the officer in the lobby, he was followed upstairs and accosted in front of the door to his room. The door opened and one of the detectives inside the room, observing . . . [Catanzaro] 'reaching for the package' under his arm, dashed from the room and grabbed him. During the ensuing struggle, in which considerable force was required to subdue . . .

[Catanzaro] the package was torn open to reveal a loaded gun. One of the officers yelled, 'I have the gun. I have the murder weapon.' ...[Catanzaro] reacted to this by blurting out, 'No, no, I was only driving the car. I didn't do it. I didn't do it. The kid did it.' In a further effort to exculpate himself ...[Catanzaro] also stated that the murder weapon was 'a .22' and that it was 'the kid' who had used it. ...[Catanzaro] was told that, if he did not co-operate, he would probably 'be stuck with this whole thing'; they 'will throw the book at you...[and] see that you get life or the chair.' He thereupon disclosed the names of his partners in crime and declared that the gun used to effect the killing had been thrown into the East River. Some time later, he gave a full statement, incriminating himself, to an assistant district attorney.''[23]

7. "...[Hicks] and White lived in a second-floor room of a rooming house. At about 5:00 a.m. on Saturday, March 20...the police responded to a report initiated by...[Hicks] that there was an unconscious man in her room. They were met by...[Hicks] who told them she could not rouse White. She told the police that White had arrived home from work Friday evening bleeding from a wound in his chest which he said he had received at the hands of some 'jitterbugs' who had jumped, robbed, and stabbed him. The police found White dead in bed with wounds in his chest and jaw. There was a small amount of blood on the undershirt and shorts he was wearing, on the sheet and blanket and on the floor between the bed and the wall. There was no sign of disorder in the room. The police found White's jacket, which had a hole corresponding with his chest wound, and his overcoat, which had blood on it but no hole.

"The police questioned...[Hicks] about White's habits, the route he would have taken home from work, his friends, associates, and debtors and about her own activities that evening. At 6:15 a.m. Detective Cannon sent other officers to verify the place of White's employment, which...[Hicks] had described as a hotel near a stated intersection, and to trace his route homeward.

"Cannon told...[Hicks] he intended to take her to the Homicide Squad Office at Police Headquarters to prepare a written report of what she had told them; she was also told she would be taken home when this was finished. Detective Cannon...did not consider...[Hicks] a suspect; in short her statements were considered plausible.

"On the way to Headquarters with...[Hicks] the police attempted to locate White's sister and made another stop to buy a package of cigarettes which...[Hicks] requested. They arrived at Headquarters at 6:40 a.m. and went to a private room in the rear of the Homicide Squad Office. ...[Hicks] was interviewed and her statement was typed in about two hours, 45 minutes being consumed by interruptions for Cannon to attend to other police business.

"Cannon asked...[Hicks] to read and sign the statement if she found it to be accurate. As she started to read it, she said she was 'in trouble.' Cannon asked what she meant by that and she responded, 'Well, it just looks like I am in trouble.' He offered her a phone to call a lawyer, assuring her that the lawyer 'will tell you that you are a witness and what you are saying is what you know about the man's death.' Shortly thereafter she signed. Cannon then offered to provide a ride home as soon as a driver was available. While they were waiting, they talked about a church where...[Hicks] had been the previous evening and with which Cannon was acquainted. In the midst of this conversation ...[Hicks] repeated her fear about being 'in trouble,' and at 9:05 a.m., she leaned forward and said 'Well, I might as well tell you, I stabbed him.'... [A]t once...[Cannon] said '[S]top right there. I want to tell you right now you are under arrest. You are charged with homicide. You are entitled to the services of a lawyer and a bondsman. You don't have to say anything. If you do, I am going to take it down and it can possibly be used against you. If you can't get your own lawyer, the Court will appoint one.'"[24]

8.   Caserino was convicted of being an accessory to a homicide. Part of the evidence against him was a statement that he made to a detective investigating the homicide during an interview in a prosecutor's office elsewhere, where he was being held on another charge. He made the incriminating statement after the detective told him that he was wanted only as a witness and that there was no intention to prosecute

him in connection with the homicide. The detective gave this assurance in good faith; the decision to prosecute Caserino was made later.[25]

9. "Schaumberg was a slot machine repairman employed at Harrah's. Cox, his brother-in-law, was visiting at Schaumberg's home. Shortly after 6:00 A.M. on September 21...Schaumberg was observed working on a dollar slot machine by a pit boss of Harrah's, Ovlan Fritz. After performing some mechanics within the machine, he adjusted it so that it was turned partially on the base plate and then left the area. Immediately thereafter, Cox went to the machine, moved it squarely onto the base plate, whereupon it registered a $5,000 jackpot. Fritz reported what he saw to two other supervisors. Together with a security guard employed by Harrah's, they asked Cox to accompany them to the security office. Leaving him in the office, they proceeded to locate Schaumberg whom they found in a washroom. Schaumberg accompanied them to the manager's office. The security guard remained outside the office while two of the supervisors, Howland and Curry, questioned Schaumberg. In all, four supervisors testified Schaumberg admitted that he had rigged the slot machine because Cox needed money."[26] The supervisors who questioned Schaumberg did not advise him of his rights. He was prosecuted for conspiracy to cheat and defraud Harrah's.

10. The defendant was indicted for murder and was arrested on a warrant charging him with that crime. Following his arrest, he offered to help the police locate a gun used in the crime. While he was riding in the police car with two detectives and trying to find the gun, he talked about the crime with them and made incriminating statements.[27]

11. Brown was arrested without a warrant on a charge of kidnapping. Before he was placed in the police car to be taken to the station, he was given *Miranda* warnings. He said that he did not want to answer any questions and wanted to talk to a lawyer. Enroute to the police station, two officers in the car discussed the kidnapping and recited the evidence against Brown but asked him no questions. The officers mentioned only evidence that they believed was in

the possession of the police. After they had talked for about ten minutes, Brown interrupted them and contradicted some of their statements. His own statements incriminated him.

Notes

1. Brown v. Mississippi, 297 U.S. 278, 286 (1936).
2. Spano v. New York, 360 U.S. 315, 317–23 (1959) (footnotes omitted).
3. *Id.* at 323.
4. Miranda v. Arizona, 384 U.S. 436 (1966).
5. *Id.* at 444 (footnote omitted).
6. Orozco v. Texas, 394 U.S. 324, 325 (1969).
7. Oregon v. Mathiason, 429 U.S. 492 (1977).
8. Rhode Island v. Innis, 446 U.S. 291, 301 (1980) (footnotes omitted).
9. Edwards v. Arizona, ___ U.S. ___ (1981).
10. North Carolina v. Butler, 441 U.S. 369 (1979).
11. Massiah v. United States, 377 U.S. 201 (1964).
12. Brewer v. Williams, 430 U.S. 387 (1977).
13. United States v. Henry, 447 U.S. 264 (1980).
14. Andresen v. Maryland, 427 U.S. 463 (1976).
15. See Fisher v. United States, 425 U.S. 391 (1976).
16. Garrity v. New Jersey, 385 U.S. 493 (1967).
17. Gardner v. Broderick, 392 U.S. 273 (1968).
18. United States v. Hall, 421 F 2d 540 (2d Cir. 1969).
19. Duffy v. State, 243 Md. 425, 429, 221 A.2d 653, 655 (1966).
20. Commonwealth v. Jefferson, 423 Pa. 541, 542–43, 226 A.2d 765, 766 (1967).
21. People v. P., 21 N.Y.2d 1, 286 N.Y.S.2d 225, 233 N.E.2d 255 (1967).
22. Brown v. Beto, 468 F.2d 1284, 1285 (5th Cir. 1972).
23. People v. Hill & Catanzaro, 17 N.Y.2d 185, 188, 269 N.Y.S.2d 422, 424–25, 216 N.E.2d 588, 590 (1966).
24. Hicks v. United States 382 F.2d 158, 160 (D.C. Cir. 1967).
25. People v. Caserino, 16 N.Y.2d 255, 265 N.Y.S.2d 644, 212 N.E.2d 884 (1965).
26. Schaumberg v. State, 83 Nev. 372, 373–74, 432 P.2d 500, 501 (1967).
27. See State v. McLeod, 1 Ohio St. 60, 203 N.E.2d 349 (1964), *summarily rev'd,* 381 U.S. 356 (1965).

CHAPTER 14

PREPARING FOR PROSECUTION

When a crime has been committed, the primary responsibility of police for the peace and order of the community is ordinarily fulfilled by an arrest. The arrest temporarily removes the apparent criminal from the community; it is also a visible indication to the victim and to people generally that the disturbing criminal event is ended and order is restored. Most likely, investigation of the crime has been or soon will be completed. Often, the investigation consists of little more than the initial response to the scene of the crime and apprehension of the criminal in circumstances that leave no doubt of his guilt. Sometimes, the arrest brings to an end a prolonged and intensive investigation. Additional investigative measures may be taken at the station immediately after the arrest. Whatever investigative pattern is followed, once an arrest has been made, police are likely to clear the crime in their own records and to regard the case as closed. From their perspective, "clearance" of the crime by arresting the criminal is the objective to be pursued.

From the larger perspective of the criminal process as a whole, an arrest typically signals not only that the investigation is completed but also that the prosecution is about to begin. Although many arrests are not followed by prosecution, the usual assumption is that an arrest is made in order to allow a prosecution to go forward. In a small number of cases, a decision to prosecute has been made and the person has been formally charged before the arrest.* While the activities of police leading to and immediately following an arrest are undertaken to fulfill their own responsibilities, officers need to be aware of the impact on prosecution and subsequent proceedings of what they do and how they do it. Application of the exclusionary rule at trial on the basis of officer's investigative practices is only one example of the close dependence of the prosecution on professional police work.

As the first and usually the only officials informed about a crime promptly after its commission, officers have a responsibility to gather information fully and accurately, and not to conclude their investigation simply because they have probable cause for an arrest. Evidence may be sufficient to clear a case and justify an arrest while leaving other questions about the crime unresolved. Investigating a homicide, for example, officers may have probable cause for an arrest despite indications that the person might have acted in self-defense. Whether or not they arrest the person, officers should try to obtain information that will help to resolve that issue. Both the prosecution and the defense are entitled to rely on officers at the scene of a crime to obtain and preserve evidence for later use. Their care in making full lists of prospective witnesses, recording statements, describing their own observations, and preparing a complete, unbiased, and informative record of all the available evidence is a principle safeguard against either a failure to convict a guilty person because evidence is lacking or a conviction of an innocent person because exculpatory evidence was lost.

It is neither practical nor desirable for officers to investigate every conceivable lead, however remote or unlikely, or however conclusive the other evidence. Having interviewed several witnesses to a crime all of whom give the same account, an officer may conclude sensibly that he need not interview a dozen remaining witnesses, if there is no reason to believe that additional information will be obtained. Officers have to make professional judgments based on their experience about which possible sources of information are likely enough

---

*See, for example, the *Spano* case, p. 161 above. Spano had been indicted for first-degree murder before he was taken into custody.

to be productive to justify a commitment of time and resources. They should be especially careful not to overlook or disregard relevant evidence because their own responsibility for clearing the case has been satisfied.

Perhaps the most common failing is to ignore apparently insignificant factual details on which important distinctions of law often depend. Although officers are not expected to have the professional competence of lawyers, they should understand the factual issues that are commonly disputed in prosecutions for the more common crimes. An officer investigating a mugging, for example, should anticipate that identification will be a critical issue if the victim thinks he could identify the mugger and no arrest was made at the scene. The officer should make a special effort to obtain a verbal description of the criminal from the victim and should carefully record the lighting conditions and other factors affecting the victim's opportunity to observe. Officers responding to the scene of a homicide should be alert to details that might indicate self-defense or to indications of homicidal intent that would affect the seriousness of the crime.

Keeping a Record

The police report of a crime is the principle investigative record. Since most cases do not go to trial, whether because the charges are finally dropped or because the defendant enters a plea of guilty, this report, which the police prepare for their own purposes, is often the only official record of the evidence that is ever made. The prosecutor, defense counsel, and often the judge may rely on the report for a summary of the facts and the evidence. An officer responsible for the preparation of a report should keep in mind these likely uses of it as well as its use by the police.

Frequently, the report is used by the lawyers and judge in the absence of the officer who prepared it. If the prosecutor and defense counsel discuss a plea of guilty, the prosecutor is likely to refer to the police report for an indication of the seriousness of the offense. The value of the report is materially increased if it is written in a concise, clear, and straightforward style and includes all information that may be relevant. Since the forms on which reports are prepared are usually designed with police uses in mind, they may not require all the information that might be useful later in the criminal process. A conscientious officer will attach additional sheets containing supplemental information. His objective, in addition to the specific objectives of his own department, should be to prepare a written account of the event that communicates effectively his own conclusions and the information on which they are based, as well as any information that might indicate a different conclusion.

Appearing as a Witness

Because officers are so often at the scene of a crime before anyone else, they are often called to testify as witnesses. Their testimony may be necessary at the trial, when the defendant's guilt is the issue, or at a preliminary proceeding, where the admission of evidence is at stake. Despite an officer's professional law-enforcement role and his professional interest in a case on which he has worked, his appearance in subsequent judicial proceedings is solely as a witness and on the same basis as other witnesses. For obvious reasons, an officer usually appears as a witness for the prosecution.

It is not surprising that officers frequently become impatient with legal proceedings or are reluctant to appear as witnesses. The proceedings may seem to exaggerate technicalities and to miss or obscure what is important because of a preoccupation with detail. An officer's irritation or frustration will be increased if the manner in which he performed his duty is attacked by the defense. It is well to recall in such circumstances that the officer's responsibilities were performed earlier and that he is not personally responsible for the outcome of the legal proceeding. If he performed his responsibilities professionally, his only concern should be to testify truthfully and accurately.

Questions for Discussion

1. Examine the crime report or incident report used in your department to record information about a crime for which an arrest is made.
    What information is required to be included?
    What additional information should normally be included?

2. What crimes are most commonly committed in your jurisdiction? (If it is important to do so, distinguish among the neighborhoods within the jurisdiction.)
    What are the elements of the crimes that are commonly committed?
    Give examples from your own experience or the experience of other officers of cases in which proof of one of the elements of a crime depended on the collection at the scene of facts that might later have become unavailable.

INDEX

About the Author

Lloyd L. Weinreb is professor of law at Harvard Law School, where he has taught courses in criminal law and criminal procedure since 1965. Before joining the faculty at Harvard, he was a federal prosecutor in the District of Columbia and law clerk to judges on the U.S. Court of Appeals for the Second Circuit and the Supreme Court of the United States. He has also been U.S. commissioner for the District of Massachusetts. An acknowledged expert on criminal justice, he has written extensively about police practices and constitutional rights, including *Denial of Justice* (1977), casebooks, and articles. He has worked closely with the police in many capacities.